LESSONS
FROM
SAINT
BENEDICT

LESSONS FROM SAINT BENEDICT

Finding Joy in Daily Life

Donald S. Raila, O.S.B.

SACRED WINDS PRESS
www.sacredwindspress.com

ISBN 978-0-9830615-4-0

Sacred Winds Press
PO Box 1
Augusta, MO 63332

Nihil Obstat:
The Reverend Monsignor Lawrence T. Persico, VG, JCL
Censor Liborum

Imprimatur:
The Most Reverend Lawrence E. Brandt, JCD, PhD
Bishop of Greensburg
Date: March 1, 2011

The *nihil obstat* and *imprimatur* are official declarations that a book or pamphlet is free of doctrinal or moral error. No implication is contained therein that those who have granted the *nihil obstat* and *imprimatur* agree with the contents, opinions or statements expressed.

Permissions and notes for images and quoted texts:

- Scripture texts in this work are taken from the *New American Bible with Revised New Testament and Revised Psalms* © 1991, 1986, 1970 Confraternity of Christian Doctrine, Washington, D.C. and are used by permission of the copyright owner. All Rights Reserved. No part of the *New American Bible* may be reproduced in any form without permission in writing from the copyright owner.
- If noted with a [†], scripture text is taken from the 1970 *New American Bible*.
- Text from the *Rule* are taken from *RB 1980: The Rule of Saint Benedict* © 1981 by Order of Saint Benedict, Inc. Published by Liturgical Press, Collegeville, Minnesota. Reprinted with permission.
- Text from *Strangers in the City* © 2005 by Michael Casey used by permission of Paraclete Press. www.paracletepress.com
- Catechism texts in this work are taken from *Catechism of the Catholic Church*. Libreria Editrice Vaticana. Paulist Press: 1994.
- Cover image: Fresco at San Marco by Fra Angelico. Image released into the Public Domain under the GNU FDL, courtesy of The Yorck Project.

10 9 8 7 6 5 4 3 2 1

*I dedicate this book to the monks of Saint Vincent Archabbey,
living and deceased, who have been helping to form me
for almost 34 years to live by the Gospel
in a Benedictine, monastic way and to find joy
in humbly surrendering my life to Christ ever more fully.*

CONTENTS

Acknowledgments

THIS book has been put together only with the cooperation of many minds and hearts. First, I thank my fellow monks at Saint Vincent Archabbey for encouraging me and challenging me over the years to cherish Christ above all and to live by the wisdom of the Rule of Saint Benedict. In particular, I thank Archabbot Douglas R. Nowicki, O.S.B., my current superior, for supporting me in my role as Director of Oblates and for permitting this book to be published with his encouragement. I thank my deceased parents, Steve and Adeline Raila, for introducing me to the faith and for setting me on a path of zealous pursuit of learning, and I am especially grateful to my mother, a high-school English teacher, for teaching me to write clearly from an early age. I am grateful, too, to the community of Oblates and Oblate novices affiliated with our Archabbey for showing me in a multitude of ways how the Rule can be lived fruitfully and joyfully by lay people. I thank our publisher, Joseph Reidhead of Sacred Winds Press, who is the son of faithful Oblates, for initiating the idea of publishing essays from Oblate newsletters in book form and for doing so much careful and valuable editing. I am grateful to Father Benedict Groeschel, C.F.R. for his willingness to write a foreword despite the many demands on his time and energy. Through his books and tapes he has been a spiritual mentor of mine for many years. Finally, I give thanks to God with all my heart, who has given me the grace both to desire to write about Benedictine values and to accomplish the writing amid various hardships. May He ever be praised!

Foreword

BY

Father Benedict J. Groeschel, CFR

Who can deny that the rule of Saint Benedict is one of the great treasures of the Church? It is a wonderfully balanced approach to growing in faith and prayerfulness, and there can be no doubt that it has brought many people closer to Christ over many centuries. Yet often we think that this rule can be employed only within the confines of the cloister. Composed by the Father of Western Monasticism over fifteen hundred years ago, the Rule of Saint Benedict may seem at first glance to be distant from our contemporary life, and we may assume that it has little to say to us. In fact, however, the exact opposite is true. The calm and balance inherent in the Rule of Saint Benedict can be of great benefit to each of us – priest, religious, or layman – as we strive to bring order and perhaps even a moment or two of peace into our relentlessly driven post-modern lives. The Rule of Saint Benedict has helped countless people in their endeavor to turn from the clamoring of the world to the serenity of God. It can help us, as well.

In *Lessons from Saint Benedict: Finding Joy in Daily Life* Fr. Donald S. Raila, OSB offers us a beautiful and gentle distillation of some of the most important elements of this magnificent rule. Drawing on his long experience as Director of Oblates at Saint Vincent Archabbey in Latrobe, Pennsylvania, he presents the Rule in a way that is not only comprehensible to contemporary lay people but is manageable by them, as well. His examples are relevant and helpful, and he is very adept at showing us how to examine our lives in terms of the Rule in a way that exposes our many foibles and failings – things that keep us separated from God but which we rarely even notice. He shows us again and again ways to recognize and eventually even overcome those things that impede our spiritual growth. This is a slender volume of meditations, but its size is deceptive. If properly used it can make a real difference in the lives of many people.

I am very pleased that Father Raila has collected some of his writings and agreed to let them be published here. I am also very excited to see that the works of Blessed Dom Columba Marmion, one of the greatest of Benedictine spiritual writers, are currently being reissued in new translations that are accessible to the modern reader. Perhaps we are seeing signs of a Benedictine renaissance, an increase in interest in the work of Saint Benedict and the great Benedictine tradition. I hope this is the case, for as Father Raila shows so well, the magnificent Rule of Saint Benedict has the potential to enrich every Christian life and to bring real and lasting joy into every Christian soul.

As a Franciscan I am very aware that my own Seraphic Father was raised by the Benedictines. Even his home parish was attached to a Benedictine abbey, and the Benedictine influence in Saint Francis's life must have been strong. It has always been my belief that these two great traditions, the Benedictine and the Franciscan, complement each other well and beautifully satisfy both the contemplative and evangelical vocations.

INTRODUCTION

IN recent decades the *Rule* of Saint Benedict (c. 480 – 547 A.D.) has become increasingly familiar to lay people who have become aware of its spiritual treasures. Some of these people, in order to enhance their lives as Christians, have taken the step of formally affiliating themselves with a Benedictine monastery by making commitments as "Oblates of Saint Benedict." As a monk with the current assignment as "Director of Oblates" affiliated with Saint Vincent Archabbey in Latrobe, Pennsylvania, I have been edified by the zeal shown by so many lay people (and secular clergy) who have made such a commitment and have lived in steadfast adherence to the values of the *Rule*, despite the fact that, when it was written about the year 530. A.D., it was intended only for a few communities of sixth-century monks. I have also realized that all of us monks and Oblates need guidance in our journeys of daily perseverance in the way of the Gospel as interpreted by the *Rule*. Thus I have been writing quarterly essays on Benedictine spirituality for some twenty-three years as part of a newsletter for Oblates, Oblate novices (those in the beginning stage of formation), and other friends of our community who have expressed interest in the Benedictine way.

The topics of my over-90 "letters" to Oblates have been scattered. As each newsletter came due, I would think of a topic based on a book that I had been reading or on a personal experience that had stirred my heart, and I would find a connection with that reading or event with a lesson from the *Rule*. I thank our publisher, Joseph Reidhead, for sifting through these essays to find those most suitable for a book and for putting those chosen into a meaningful sequence. I thank him, too, for compiling an index of themes so that the reader can either read the whole book through as it is written or else seek out the chapters that address themes that are most relevant in his or her life.

For the reader not familiar with the basic terms of Benedictine life, I should perhaps give a brief explanation. First of all, the *Rule* of

Saint Benedict—not so much a set of rules as a book of Christian wisdom for people living in community—is a document of rich spiritual meaning despite its ancient date. It draws heavily from Scripture and is totally Christ-centered. Some of the chapters, such as those dealing with penalties and "excommunication," may at first glance seem hopelessly out-of-touch with our modern world. However, although the precepts of such chapters are no longer followed literally even in monasteries, they embody such valuable lessons as personal accountability and the urgent need to correct disorders and offenses with charity and swiftness.

The *Rule* prescribes a balanced schedule of community prayer, individual prayer, and manual labor. The prayer in community, called "Opus Dei" (Latin for the Work of God) or the Divine Office, is now generally called the Liturgy of the Hours. In Saint Benedict's day it was prayed eight times a day. These days some contemplative monasteries still gather for the "Office" seven or eight times each day whereas more active communities like my own gather only three times. In its varied forms the Divine Office remains the official "prayer of the Church," and many Oblates and other lay people have found nourishment in praying the Office at least one time a day, as their schedules allow. In the tradition of the *Rule*, the private prayer of the monk consisted largely of *lectio divina*, a slow, meditative pondering of the Bible or writings of the Church fathers. *Lectio*, too, has been growing in popularity in recent years and is sometimes practiced in small groups. Finally, the dimension of work remains significant as a way to exercise one's God-given gifts for the good of others. The work which was generally limited to manual labor in Saint Benedict's day can now take the form of intellectual work or ministry by monks. The principles of the *Rule* regarding work can easily be applied by lay people to whatever legitimate work in which they are engaged.

The vows taken by the monks in Saint Benedict's day as well as our day (see Chapter 58 of the *Rule*) are stability, obedience, and *conversatio morum*. Stability binds a monk to a particular monastic community for life. Obedience binds the monk to heed God's voice through superiors, other monks, the Word of God, and the situations of daily life. *Conversatio*, perhaps the most mysterious of the three vows, is translated in various ways. It basically challenges the monk to live in persevering fidelity to an authentic monastic lifestyle. It challenges him, too, to live in ongoing conversion as he does his part to conform his life to Christ in a monastic way. This entails humility since one can never say on this earth, "I have done enough; I have advanced in spiritual life as far as I need to."

These vows are readily applicable to lay Christians. All Christians can live in stability when they remain firmly rooted in Christ amid the vicissitudes of daily life. All Christians can live in obedience by listening for God's voice in the Scriptures, in the teachings of Christ and the Church, in the needs of other people, in prayer, and in the circumstances of ordinary life. All Christians can live in *conversatio morum* by fulfilling their baptismal commitment. In the waters of baptism a new Christian dies to his or her old, self-centered way of life and rises to new life in Christ. The monastic life is basically an intensification of one's baptismal commitment. Lay people who aspire to live by the *Rule* thus "die to self" daily and put on a new, Christ-centered way of life. Again and again, they are summoned by God to lay aside old ways that do not conform to one's Christian calling and to embrace new ways that help one to live zealously by the Gospel. Following the *Rule* often opens people to daily opportunities, in generally small, unpretentious ways, to die to self and rise with Christ and to persevere joyfully in this strenuous endeavor.

Yes, the process should be joyful in the sense that we Christians have come to understand the word "joy." Genuine joy is an essential part of Christian life. My own understanding of Christian joy has been strongly influenced by the doctoral dissertation entitled *Joy in Lent* by one of our monks, Father Kurt Belsole, O.S.B. That document reminds us that joy in the *Rule* and in Christian life is an inner disposition and a fruit of the Holy Spirit (cf. Gal 5:22). Joy is not mere "happiness," which in its historical origins and in its usual meaning depends on circumstances and is a matter of emotional contentment. Joy, on the other hand, can coexist with sorrow and great suffering because it entails gratitude for the redeeming work of Christ. As Father Kurt points out, the fact that the *Rule's* two references to joy occur in Chapter 49, which is about Lent and in which it is stated that a monk's life should be a "continuous Lent" (*Rule* 49:1), indicates that the whole of a monk's life should be joyful. Thus the whole *Rule* is, in a sense, about Christian joy. (It is interesting, also, that a single mention of "rejoicing" occurs in Chapter 7, in the context of "obedience under difficult, unfavorable, or even unjust conditions." Saint Benedict thus tells us that this joy emerges from the trust in God's reward and confidence in Christ's love, shown to us most powerfully on the Cross.) Our true and lasting joy is our communion with Christ. As in the case of Saint John the Baptist, we find this joy reaching completion when Christ increases in us and when we (that is, our autonomous, unredeemed selves) decrease (cf. John 3:30).

Coping with life can often be difficult, whether one is Christian or not. In this age of widespread ignorance of or contempt for traditional Judeo-Christian values and of overemphasis on science and human reason, we can easily lose sight of God's graces and become discouraged. However, amid all the stresses and tragedies of modern life, the Gospel and the *Rule* summon us to live in joy. On the surface we may see ourselves only as rising from bed, eating, working, dealing with other people (sometimes with very difficult personalities), recreating, resting, and trying to manage seemingly unbearable burdens. Beneath the surface of these human activities we can learn to see, with the guidance of the Gospel and the *Rule*, that every dimension of our lives is overflowing with God's lavish graces, is leading us to rejoice in His love, and is renewing us in that love, perhaps especially when we feel forsaken and hopeless. We can learn to "rejoice always" (cf. 1 Thes 5:16) because Christ is with us always to save us, to transform us, and to draw us into eternal life with our loving Father and all the saints. Christ, in fact, is our Joy. It is my hope and my prayer that Oblates and others who read this book will discover the joy hidden in daily life because Christ is there to set us free. May this little volume lead the reader to find immense spiritual riches in the "little rule" of Saint Benedict and in ordinary life situations so that we may also more and more discover the joy of welcoming Christ to become everything in all of us.

1

⬤⬤

THE RULE:
NOT A FORMULA FOR GOOD ORDER
BUT A WAY TO LIVE IN GOD'S ORDER

W HEN people apply to be invested as Oblate novices, they often express the hope that following the *Rule* of Saint Benedict and becoming affiliated with our monastic community will help to bring some stability into their unruly lives. Some are attracted to the commitment to pray the Divine Office and to practice *lectio divina* because such practices may put some order into their prayer lives. Indeed, in our society many people, Christian or not, suffer from inner and outer instability and lack of healthful order. Dysfunctional family situations, stress at work, excessive workloads, and economic anxieties—not to mention each individual's own sinful inclinations—can all contribute to a deficiency of peace and order in life. When people are driven by desires to succeed, to have pleasure, to please others, or to have some relief from burdens, they can become trapped in a frantic quest for happiness that can never be fulfilled. Sometimes efforts to satisfy disordered desires can render them more unruly and enslaving. Affiliation with a monastery may seem appealing as a possible way to find peace amid the chaos of daily life.

⁓

I suppose that I myself entered the monastery partly out of a desire to put more order and stability into my prayer life. The ideal of a steady monastic routine, with regular times for prayer and nicely ordered work, seemed to provide a welcome alternative to the often frantic patterns of work in graduate school and in the work place. Are not monasteries known to function like clockwork, with peace flowing from fixed times for community prayer, private prayer, meals, work, and recreation? Do not monasteries provide a virtually guaranteed way to holiness through the regularity of time-tested monastic routines?

There is some truth to the notion that the *Rule* and its embodiment in a community of like-minded people should provide a well-ordered way to salvation and sanctification. However, order alone is not sufficient to bring us closer to God, for His grand order, as revealed by Jesus Christ, is vastly beyond our sense of order. In fact, Our Lord frequently took the Pharisees to task for trying to create an air-tight spiritual order that seemed to guarantee their abiding in righteousness, but which in fact excluded the living God and prevented the practice of heartfelt charity to tax-collectors, lepers, and others whom the Pharisees considered beyond the realm of God's care.

Ꮿ

We can all slip into the trap of seeking "good order" for its own sake. As someone who has a long-standing and sometimes fanatic desire for order, I certainly can do that. For some months our community has been revising our version of the Divine Office, and I have been responsible for some of the typing of psalms and the inserting of musical notations. During the weeks before the deadline for our new format (and during the several weeks after), life was especially frantic for those of us monks on the Liturgy Committee. As a result, the new psalters for Morning Prayer and Midday Prayer were printed with many errors, many of which arose from my hastiness and neglect. I am sorely tempted to fret, "If only I had been more careful, if only I had taken more time to proofread, if only I had been calmer when I typed, there would not have been such disorder in the psalters!" At the same time, I realize more and more that no matter how hard

I try, I shall continue to make errors and that while the yearning for good order can be helpful, it can also be perfectionistic, obsessive, and therefore self-centered. A relevant contemporary saying is, "Anything worth doing is worth doing badly."[1] That is, despite all our momentous efforts to make things "perfect," our work will always be poor and imperfect, especially in contrast with God's flawless ways. However, that is not the whole story. In our weakness God is strong, and His good order of compassion, forgiveness, and selfless love more than makes up for our human deficiencies. When we surrender our poor efforts to Christ, they can become channels of lavish graces for others and ourselves. When we let go of our limited human sense of order to welcome God's order of self-emptying love, He can produce far better results than the "perfect" outcomes for which we strive. In our case of the revised psalters, the need to correct dozens of errors necessitated teams of novices and volunteers to tape in corrections; and their cheerful embracing of routine was edifying to me. Perhaps the whole tedious process gave us all a better sense of the care that we monks are to show for our Divine Office.

∽

In the *Rule*, Saint Benedict, on numerous occasions, clearly states that he wants good order in his monasteries.

∽

Some of the older monks in our community have passed down the saying, "Keep the *Rule*, and the *Rule* will keep you." In other words, the *Rule* itself is a sure formula for living a good monastic life; so heeding it is practically an automatic way to unimpeded spiritual progress. That statement has some truth, but much depends on what one means by "keeping the *Rule*." Again, the *Rule* is not a set of rules or a collection of inflexible regulations; it is not so for monks today, and it is certainly not so for Oblates. "Keeping the *Rule*" is, therefore, not to be construed as a literal adherence to its prescriptions. Likewise, our efforts to fulfill requirements, whether literal or not,

---

1   G.K. Chesterton. *What's Wrong with the World*

cannot of themselves bring us to a proper relationship with God. However, God can and does use our readiness to follow the time-tested wisdom of the *Rule* to deepen our daily, lived-out commitment to Christ. A genuine "keeping of the *Rule*" in spirit, with reliance on God's grace, can continually draw us back to our vocation to be children of God amid life's uncertainties, interruptions, and bumpy relationships and amid our own sinfulness. There is no hard-and-fast formula for salvation, but the *Rule* does provide a stable, time-tested way for opening one's being to the daily call of God that beckons one to a growing, vibrant fellowship with Christ.

❧

The *Rule* is a document of spiritual wisdom that, taken all together, can help to open the human heart to the mystery of God Himself.

❧

Besides calling for "good order," the *Rule* itself tells us that there will always be disorders in monastic (and Oblate) communities and that even (in an ideal community) when there is "good order," God's order draws us beyond our limited human conception of order, valid though it may be as a way to live the Gospel. It seems that monks in Saint Benedict's monasteries regularly disrupted the ideal order. It was known that monks would "presume to defend their own views obstinately"[2] at community meetings. Some monks even presumed to contend with their abbot.[3] Saint Benedict had to legislate for restraint of speech[4] because there were occasions when monks used "vulgarity and gossip."[5] Throughout the *Rule* there are descriptions of disordered situations that Saint Benedict must have encountered in his monasteries, and surely these were not instantly corrected by a simple application of regulations. The passages about the Divine Office may be especially pertinent regarding this matter. After prescribing the

---

2   *RB 1980: The Rule of Saint Benedict* [henceforth RB]: 3:4
3   RB 3:9
4   RB 6
5   RB 6:8

arrangement for Sunday Vigils in great detail,[6] Saint Benedict mentions that it "should be followed at all times, summer and winter, unless—God forbid—the monks happen to arise too late. In that case, the readings or responsories will have to be shortened."[7] He likewise instructs the monks that at the beginning of Vigils, Psalm 95 should be "said quite deliberately and slowly"[8] since any monk who arrived after the concluding "Glory be" was to be punished. Thus, while Saint Benedict loathes the disorders of late rising and late attendance and has prescribed penalties for such lateness, he also expresses charity in his readiness both to shorten readings (to avoid monks' suffering from an excessively prolonged Office) and to do what he can to keep stragglers from being officially late. Above all, charity must prevail! Perhaps God's order may even require a certain amount of human disorder. The breaking in of His love often demands the superseding of human norms, the embracing of inconvenience, and sometimes even the enormous sacrifice of well laid-out plans so that He can overcome our prideful attachment to apparently water-tight schemes for satisfaction and salvation. He must teach us, too, that we are not self-sufficient.

☙

Again and again in my own monastic life, I am slowly learning to let go of my inner insistence for *my* order so that I may welcome the love of Christ to prevail in any given situation. When I see items out of place or missing, I tend to think, "Why can't people put things back where they belong? Why can't people return what they borrow?" Although it is natural to ask such questions and to be concerned about others' lack of responsibility, it can lead to sinful preoccupations and judgments. How much better it is to turn to the Lord and pray, "Lord, show me how I can cheerfully and lovingly put things back into order? Lord, how can missing things give me an opportunity for personal encounters with some of your children? Lord, put Your good order of love into my heart where there is frustration and

6   RB 7
7   RB 11:11-12
8   RB 43:4

bitterness!" Likewise, when things go wrong in the monastic choir, I am tempted to fret, "Why didn't I put out enough extra booklets for our abundant guests?" or "Why do all these imperfect situations keep me from being prayerful at liturgy?" Should I not rather offer all these disorders to Christ and say, "Thank You, Lord, that we are all here. Thank You for those who put out extra booklets where I failed. Lord, help me to turn to You for mercy and forgiveness for myself and others, and to set my heart on You now instead of letting all these problems lead my heart to disorder and distraction."

❧

In the lives of Oblates, living their radical commitment in the world, the Lord likewise provides frequent opportunities to prefer His order of charity to our limited sense of good order. Of course, we do need to be firm about establishing a minimal amount of order in our lives, especially if they tend to be undisciplined and chaotic. Only with such order can we avoid mortal sin, be eager to follow the teachings of Christ and the Church, and open ourselves to hear God's word. If, as in Our Lord's parable about the sower of the seed, we provide only a footpath or rocky ground or thorns and thistles, then we had better work at our attitudes and environment to render ourselves better disposed to obey God. Beyond that, however, we need to be cautious of clinging to our well-established order. We need to be ready to surrender to God's order. When others take more of our time than we expect, we must extend ourselves in charity, at least for a little while. When others have misplaced items that we need, our reminders to them should be marked by patience and personal concern. When we become frustrated over our own errors, we need to bring to the Lord our fallibility, vulnerability, and littleness and seek the grace to rely on Him more instead of trusting in our own mental and physical skills. Even regarding our sins, while we do need to repent and to struggle to do better every day, we also need to accept our poor selves in all their miseries and disorders and then welcome Christ to bring us the healing and forgiveness that He so desires to lavish upon us.

❧

Yes, our sense of good order can reflect God's all-wise plan for us, but His order of love involves far more. Christ's rule of love must be allowed to prevail over even our best laid-out plans. Stability does not mean standing still, but remaining firm in Christ so that He may do with us as He wills. The vow of stability is necessarily coupled with the vow of *conversatio morum,* whereby we welcome the Lord to "turn" us over and over again to render us purer recipients and vehicles of His grace. Stability thus beckons us to embrace the Cross and "to stand fast, even to endure joyfully whatever may come" (Col 1:11†). Ultimately, there will never be a perfect order in this world, although we should indeed work for an increasingly better order. Rather, "what we await are new heavens and new earth where, according to his promise, the justice of God will reside" (2 Pt 3:13†).

2

---⊗⊗⊗---

SEEKING THE TRUTH THAT SETS US FREE

ALL of us long for freedom. We long to be free from the constraints that keep us from becoming the people we are meant to be. We long for the freedom to lead joyful, fulfilling, purpose-filled lives. However, sometimes we seek an illusory freedom that is more akin to destructive self-indulgence or judgmental self-justification. What, then, is true freedom from a Christian perspective?

For one who lives in Christ there is no freedom that focuses merely on oneself and one's desires; there is no freedom without a reaching out to God and a reaching out to others in love. During the Christmas Season we celebrate the coming of God as man to set us free from sin and death and to render us free to share in His divine life of love. Thus it is God who defines what human freedom is since it is He who created us, redeemed us, and sanctifies us. Looking at the earthly life of our incarnate Lord, we can see that He continually responded to the Father's love with a succession of acts of self-emptying love that were intended to free us to know that love and to believe in that love. In the Office of Readings for the Tuesday after Epiphany, we hear in a sermon on the Epiphany, "By his passion [inflicted on him by others], he frees us from the passions [unleashed by our disobedience]; by receiving a blow on the cheek he gives the world its liberty; by being pierced in the side he heals the wound of Adam... To give us a new birth that would make our bodies and souls immortal, he breathed into us the spirit of life and armed us with

incorruptibility."[1] What a grace! What a blessing! Indeed we have a
longing for freedom; but as we see in the life of Our Lord, the price
of obtaining freedom is great. Are we willing to enter into the baptismal waters again and again to be cleansed of sin, to surrender our
lives to Christ, and to live in unrelenting sacrificial love? That is true
freedom: to live in persistent communion with Christ, who is the
One who sets us free.

∾

What, then, is the Christian freedom that all of us disciples of
Christ seek? The Scriptures speak about freedom both from passions
and attachments and from human-imposed restrictions that can in-
terfere with our openness to God. In particular, Saint Paul addresses
the issue of freedom in Christ and refers to it as "life in the Spirit."
He tells the Galatians, "It was for liberty that Christ freed us. So
stand firm, and do not take on yourselves the yoke of slavery a second
time!" (Gal 5:1[†]). Later he continues, "Remember that you have been
called to live in freedom—but not a freedom that gives free rein to
the flesh. Out of love, place yourselves at one another's service" (Gal
5:13[†]). In other words, Christian freedom involves the capacity to
be who God meant us to be: children of a loving Father who delight
in His love, who follow the law of the Spirit rather than the law of
the flesh, and who generously and cheerfully serve others in love—
the same self-emptying love that Christ offered to the world in His
ministry, Passion, and death. It is freedom to know Christ's love, to
remain in a communion of love with Him, and to manifest that love.
As the Christmas hymn "God Rest You Merry, Gentlemen" states in
verse 4:

> *"Fear not, then," said the angel, "Let nothing you affright*
> *This day is born a Savior of a pure Virgin bright,*
> *To free all those who trust in Him from Satan's pow'r and might."*

---

1   This excerpt is from a sermon on the Epiphany (nn. 2.6-8 10: PG 10, 854.
858-859. 862) attributed to Saint Hippolytus, an Early Church Father, is used in the
Roman Office of Readings for Tuesday between the Feast of the Epiphany and the Feast
of the Baptism of the Lord.

Satan's power shows itself both in slavery to passions and in rigid adherence to self-chosen regulations. Both types of behavior close us off from the graces of God and thus enslave us to living on a sensual or self-justifying level.

In Book Three of Pope Saint Gregory the Great's *Dialogues*, there appears a hermit, Martin, who had chained himself to a rock inside his narrow cave. Apparently, Martin thought he was performing a good and holy act of asceticism. When Abbot Benedict heard about Martin, he "sent word to him that the love of Christ should keep him chained there instead of the iron chain he was using."[2] The hermit heeded the abbot's advice. This incident shows that acts of self-denial are not always freeing. They can be the result of pride, and they can bind us in slavery to self-will rather than in the servanthood of Christ's love, which is true freedom. The life of a Christian indeed requires that he "deny his very self, take up his cross, and follow in [Christ's] steps" (Mk 8:34[†]); but the self-denial must be one given by God and performed out of love for Christ and others.

It is this kind of self-denial and genuine freedom that people seek—I hope—when they apply to our Oblate Program. They want to become freer persons. Many state that they hope that the *Rule* will give them the salutary structure and discipline they need to pursue a more committed Christian life. Yes, it is paradoxically true that self-discipline and self-denial, when chosen in response to God's word, become means to freedom! Also, many applicants assert that they seek the support of a living community of faith that can lead them to a fuller life of prayer and loving service, and they hope that the Oblate community will fulfill this role.

℘

The *Rule* of Saint Benedict does assist its followers to walk in the freedom of God's children and, therefore, to strive for a holiness that is characterized by a constant abiding in Christ's love. Although the word "free" (*liber* in Latin) does not appear frequently in the *Rule*, the whole tenor of the document is that of binding oneself to a way

---

2   *Life and Miracles of St. Benedict*, translated by Odo J Zimmerman, O.S.B. and Benedict R. Avery, O.S.B. Liturgical Press: Collegeville, MN, p. xi

of life that frees one to follow Christ and His Gospel. Right at the outset, the Prologue summons the monk to accept the advice of a loving father "willingly"[3] (*libenter* in Latin); such free, willing obedience helps the monk to return to the Father from whom he has so often drifted. One of the instruments of good works is to "listen [willingly] to holy reading";[4] such reading—*holy reading* is a translation of *lectio divina*—frees one to know Christ and live in Him. When Saint Benedict speaks of *lectio*, he sometimes uses the term *lectioni vacant*[5] or *vacant lectionibus*[6]. The Latin *vacant* comes from the verb *vacare*, which means to become empty or free. The monastic life frees up time to enable the Word of God to permeate one's life. It is interesting that our word "vacation" comes from the same root word; the Latin *vacatio* means "freedom" or "exemption." Our true *vacation* is not a license to do whatever we please but rather the freedom to use all our time and energy to become better disciples, to "run and do now what will profit us forever."[7] In Prol: 43, Saint Benedict uses the word *vacat* in the phrases "there is still time" and "have time"; that is, all of us who follow the *Rule* need to strive constantly to be emptied of selfish concerns so that we might in all things hasten more quickly to Christ and to our heavenly home.

એન

Our participation in the Divine Office also serves to free us for formation by God's Word, which *washes over us* every time we pray the psalms and the accompanying readings, even if we do not grasp every word intellectually. Furthermore, there is the discipline of dropping everything else and going to pray when the literal or figurative bell rings to summon the monk or Oblate to pray the Divine Office. Such a routine frees us from being consumed by our work and other concerns in order to put God first in our lives. (The Divine Office is

---

3   According to the translations by Abbot Parry, O.S.B.
4   RB 4:55
5   RB 48:10
6   RB 48:13, 14
7   RB Prologue:44

meant to do just that as it assists us to consecrate to God this hour of the day and ultimately all moments of the day.)

~

How, then, can we followers of Saint Benedict become truly free? Christ and the Church call to be "free from" and "free for." First, we are to be more and more liberated from disordered impulses. Saint Benedict recommends, "He [the faithful monk] has foiled the evil one, the devil, at every turn, flinging both him and his promptings far from the sight of his heart. While these temptations were still young, he caught hold of them and dashed them against Christ."[8] Again he urges us, "As soon as wrongful thoughts come into your heart, dash them against Christ and disclose them to your spiritual father."[9] "Temptations," the devil's promptings, and "wrongful thoughts" can include self-indulgent thoughts, judgmental thoughts, prideful thoughts, despairing thoughts, envious or jealous thoughts, uncaring thoughts, spiteful thoughts, or vengeful thoughts. All of these, if we indulge in them, enslave us by cutting us off from the grace of God, who is pure love. Insofar as we at any time are surprised by such thoughts (or even find ourselves generating them deliberately), we need to catch ourselves as soon as possible and to welcome Christ to set us free from such threats. This freedom is generally gained only over a long period of time, perhaps only after a lifelong struggle.

Secondly, adhering to a daily structure that includes time for the Liturgy of the Hours and *lectio divina* is another safeguard against the tendency to drift away from God's will and into whatever strikes our fancy. Freeing up time for these practices exposes us to the Word of God, which judges us, comforts us, and transforms us into the children of God that we are meant to be. Obedience to the Word frees us from the tyranny of self-will. Although we may know God's will in a general way from the teachings of the Church and the Scriptures, discovering His specific will for ourselves in a particular circumstance requires extra effort. It is *lectio divina* that is specifically geared to expose us to God's very personal word for us as we listen intently in

---

8   RB Prologue:28
9   RB 4:50

silence to the Word in Scripture. Practicing *lectio* and praying the Divine Office can form us in a habit of listening for God's Word in every circumstance. Such frequent immersion in the Word disposes us to abide in the truth that comes from God and that sets us free (Jn 8:32†). In fact, Christ is the Truth who sets us free; as He says, "If the Son frees you, you will really be free" (Jn 8:36†).

Finally, becoming truly free necessarily involves other people, especially members of Christ's Body. Several months ago I had a splinter in a knuckle on my right hand. It was something small but potentially dangerous. At first I did not recognize the dark spot as a splinter of wood. Once I did, however, I saw that I could not remove it myself, especially since I am right-handed. I then went to ask the nurse on duty in our infirmary to remove the splinter and thus to free me from the danger of infection. When afterwards I went to pray before the Blessed Sacrament, I felt moved by the thought that it is much harder to remove the splinters (or planks!) of sins and bad habits from my heart. To eradicate these I need not only *lectio*, the Office, the monastic routine, and the guidance of the *Rule*, but also, and very essentially, the loving, corrective support of a spiritual director and a whole faith-community to keep me struggling against slavery to sin and against whatever prevents me from growing into a fuller life in Christ.

❧

Let us acknowledge that in many ways we are still unfree. Let us yearn more and more for the freedom that Our Lord wishes to bestow on us. Let us use the prayerful means He has given us to overcome the slavery of living in the flesh, and let us welcome His grace that frees us to live in the Spirit. Let us also support one another in communities of faith so that together we may more fully come to know the truth that sets us free (Jn 8:32†)!

3

RUNNING LATE OR RUNNING TO GOD?
LEARNING TO WELCOME TIME AS HIS GIFT

RUSHING, running late, and running out of time can become acceptable modes of operation for many of us. Does not our culture encourage us to prove ourselves by being busy (and therefore by rushing mindlessly from one task to the next) and by showing ourselves important (and therefore by running late because our tasks are so utterly urgent)? If our tasks weren't urgent, then there would be something wrong; we might not be as indispensable as we would like to think, and then we might feel worthless and become depressed and have "too much time on our hands"; heaven forbid! On the other hand, when our mind is racing ahead to the next important event or task, are we really giving enough attention to the situation at hand? If we are thinking only about what is to come, then does not such an attitude render the present time somewhat meaningless? Likewise, if we become so immersed in a given activity that we dread the possibility of interruption, then are we not trying frantically to control time on our own terms and failing to nurture our capacity to serve others in love? If we are captured in any of these attitudes and behaviors, then perhaps we might better consider the alternative of *running to God*—and to His gracious will for us.

❧

For several months I had been driving on the road more than usual, partly because of vacation time and partly because of some

long-distance weekend missions, not to speak of visits to Oblates
in Williamsport and Lancaster. Thanks to spiritual conferences on
cassette tapes, which I almost always bring along with me, I was generally relaxed as I drove. Observing other vehicles on the road, I had
the impression that most people who are traveling are in a hurry,
and I sometimes wondered what was running through their minds.
Are their lives necessarily frantic? If so, are they happy about living
in a frantic mode? Are they typically "running behind schedule" and
worrying about arriving late? In rushing to get from one place to another, are they regarding time spent on the road as wasted time to be
hurried through as quickly as possible? Are they concerned about the
disposition of their hearts and minds, or do they judge it natural to
be anxious, hurried, and frenzied? How do they regard fellow travel-
ers in other vehicles—if they think about them at all as humans like
themselves?

❧

Before thus speculating about others' thoughts, perhaps I had best
look to my own. Do I practice—or at least struggle to practice—what
I preach? Sometimes not! Despite spiritual nourishment from tapes
and occasional classical music from the radio and despite my cus-
tom of beginning journeys amply early, I still find my mind running
in disordered ways. Instead of resting in the present moment, my
thoughts often rush ahead to what I must do when I reach my destination. "What shall I do the moment I arrive? If I arrive a bit early,
then perhaps I can squeeze in a bit more prayer or a phone call or the
nap that I might need. If I arrive later than I would like (and may that
not happen!), then I may be in trouble; I might have to hurry to the
Divine Office without unpacking or play the organ at Office without practicing or... No, there must not be any further delay because
of red lights or construction or slow trucks or school buses!" How
damaging such thoughts can be, and how far removed they are from
a serene mindfulness of God! It is not only on the road that I can
allow my thoughts to run in the wrong direction. Even when I am
writing letters in my office, I can easily begin to worry and scheme
how many more paragraphs I can complete before I leave for Midday

Prayer. When I am eating lunch, I can start plotting how I can finish quickly and thus cram more tasks into the allotted time in the afternoon, which always seems too short. When I am practicing the violin (which is supposed to be recreation), I can slip into worrying how soon I shall finish playing the current piece so that I may have more time to enjoy the one that is coming up. Thus my mind (and perhaps yours) can form the habit of running and rushing to the next event, even when such thoughts are totally unnecessary. I may even begin to regard myself as a pitiable victim who is always falling behind and running out of time. Thus there seems always to be too much to do. There is no occasion to savor the present moment or activity because I must mentally rush onward to the next one; otherwise I might lose my control over time and fail to direct it to my own self-gratifying goals, and things would only grow worse (since it is I who know best how to schedule my time!). However, what happens to the grace of the moment or to the person whom I am called to serve here and now or to the word of God sown in my heart at the present time, which He so lovingly desires to get across to me?

℘

The *Rule* of Saint Benedict and its spiritual practices can help us to be freed from the frantic, restless cycle of running late and then seeking relief in mindless, self-gratifying distractions. Rather than to run mentally or physically to gain control over agendas that are falling miserably behind schedule, we are urged to run to God. The Prologue exhorts us to "run while you have the light of life,"[1] to "run [to the tent of God's Kingdom] by doing good deeds,"[2] to "run and do now what will profit us forever,"[3] and to hope to "run on the path of God's commandments, our hearts overflowing with the inexpressible delight of love."[4] The abbot is to help the other monks run to God; in his concern for the wayward brothers, for example, he himself is to "act with all speed, discernment, and diligence in order

---

1   RB Prologue:13, Jn 12:35
2   RB Prologue:22
3   RB Prologue:44
4   RB Prologue:49

not to lose any of the sheep entrusted to him."[5] Regarding communal prayer, all the monks, "on hearing the signal for an hour of the
Divine Office,"... are to "go with utmost speed" to the choir chapel.[6]
In all these situations, the monk is summoned to run in response to
God's word. So eager is Saint Benedict to have his monks heed the
call of God above all else that he changes Saint John's word "walk"[7] to
"run."[8] That is, whenever God sheds His light upon a situation, the
monk is to hasten to go in the indicated direction as his first priority. The most urgent task in the monk's—or any Christian's—life is
to hurry gracefully to fulfill God's will in every situation. The call
of God is so important that "the monk will immediately set aside
[whatever other things] he has in hand"[9] and "put aside [his] own
concerns" and "abandon [his] own will"[10] to follow whatever command the Lord is giving him. This command, of course, is not a
military-like order that God imposes in order to assert His authority.
Rather, it is a loving invitation to enter into Christ's own divine life
and to grow into a supremely fulfilling relationship with God, which
is the greatest treasure we could possibly have.

❧

How, in practical ways, can we overcome our tendency to run
mindlessly to self-seeking goals? How can we free ourselves to run to
God with the good zeal that will overflow into enhanced relationships
with others? For one thing, we can start by learning to appreciate
time as God's gift and not a commodity over which we exert control
willy-nilly; we are stewards of time and not lords over it. The fact
that we so often exhaust ourselves in frantic attempts to control time
should help us to realize that we were not meant to be totally in control of it. The practice of praying the Liturgy of the Hours implies
that we hand over that specific time, and ultimately all times of the
day, to God for His own purposes, which sometimes differ from ours.

---

5   RB 27:5
6   RB 43:1
7   RB from Jn 12:35
8   RB Prologue:13
9   RB 43:1
10   RB 5:7

For us vowed religious, the Divine Office is meant particularly to interrupt whatever else we are doing, and we are committed by vow to hasten to join the community for the Hours unless illness, distance, or assigned pastoral need takes us away. For lay people the praying of the Hours must be subservient to ordinary charitable duties; but even so, when one, with proper discernment, does make time to pray an Hour, it may still be felt as an intrusion, and that may be a good thing. Especially if the alternative is a self-chosen, more pleasurable activity, we may be called to overcome the false guilt that sometimes comes along with making time for God. We may be called to welcome the intrusion that is His gift, a gift that helps us run to Him. Likewise, our entering into *lectio divina* hands over a portion of time explicitly to God with the intent of our hearing His word in the Scriptures or other inspirational writings. That life-giving word may very well set us running in new directions if we carry God's message with us through the day. These forms of prayer, coupled with the moment-by-moment effort to nurture humility, to maintain a silent heart, and to live in attentiveness to God's ongoing call, can help us to view time more and more as *kairos*, the sacred time that celebrates God's saving action among us, and less and less as mere *chronos*, the temporal succession of seconds, days, and years that we struggle to harness for our self-chosen endeavors.

Immersion in *kairos*, or "God's time," can make a big difference in the ways we respond to situations. Here are a few possible examples:

(1) When I "begin a good work,"[11] I may pray at the outset that I leave the result in God's hands rather than frantically aim to achieve the success that I have in mind.

(2) When I encounter slow traffic or a tie-up of vehicles on the road and find no way out of it, then I can "open [my] eyes to the light that comes from God"[12] and thank Him for letting my will be challenged; I can ask Him to slow down my racing heart and impulsive mind so that I may take a moment to pray for the other drivers and for those responsible for the delay, especially if there are victims of an accident. Furthermore, if I chronically tend to exceed the speed limit,

11   RB Prologue:4
12   RB Prologue:9

I might ask myself whether such a habit betrays a lack of trust in God. If it is His will that I generally obey the laws of the land, including traffic laws, then will He not enable me to arrive at the right place at the right time if I travel within the prescribed speed limit?

(3) When I encounter people who seem slow to learn or slow to respond to my seemingly urgent needs, I might consider that God's timetable for others to develop may differ from my expectations. Like the good abbot, I must know that I am called to serve "a variety of temperaments, coaxing, reproving, and encouraging them as appropriate";[13] but, above all, I am challenged to have reverence for the unique dignity of all people and to use time to enhance that dignity in whatever ways God may provide.[14] My choice to be ruled by impulsiveness and impatience can be downright uncharitable because it detracts from others' capacity to seek God in peace and at the pace that is right for them.

(4) When I am doing one thing and my mind begins to run to a thousand other possibilities, I can gently refocus on this moment and this task and these people in front of me. I can implore the Lord to help me to "seek first the kingdom of God," and He will provide the resources necessary to accomplish all the other tasks that need to be done. Such refocusing may need to be repeated over and over.

(5) When I am tempted to rush hastily to "defend [my] own views obstinately"[15] in the presence of others, I can recall that the Lord speaks some significant truth through the various opinions of others. He "often reveals what is better to the younger,"[16] or to the poorer and the apparently less intelligent and less proficient. It is time for me to slow down my racing, opinionated mind in order to revere the other and listen to the other and perhaps even to welcome a change of heart and mind.

(6) Now and then I want time to go more slowly. If I am waiting in a doctor's office and begin to do some reading that I have brought along, I typically desire that I won't be called until I finish a certain

---

13   RB 2:31
14   RB 2:33-36
15   RB 3:4
16   RB 3:3

chapter. If I am waiting for a guest and bring some correspondence to work on while I am waiting, I tend to wish that the guest not arrive until I finish writing a certain letter. What self-important ways we have of trying to manipulate time! In such cases I again need to ward off self-centered desires, to surrender my use of time to God's own loving purpose, and to spring up joyfully, inwardly and outwardly, at the moment I am called to greet my guest or to see the doctor. Will not such prompt "running to God" have a positive effect on those whom I meet?

✧

In sum, the sacredness of the gift of time challenges us to welcome each moment as coming from the hands of our loving Father, who sent His Son into the world to sanctify all things, including time. To develop such a disposition, we must be healed of tendencies to grasp time for our own self-fulfilling purposes, to neglect valuing the "wasted time" between events and destinations, and to run late continually because we try to force too many projects into too short a time. Instead, let us run to Christ as His "little ones" who open themselves to Christ's marvelous revelation; let us find "rest" in the Lord Jesus Himself, rather than in our own achievements, and become "meek and humble of heart" like Him (cf. Mt 11:25-30). Through our *lectio divina*, our praying of the Divine Office, and our efforts to practice the presence of God at all times, we may receive the grace to praise God for the lavish gifts of the present moment and recognize, with Saint Paul, that "now is a very acceptable time... now is the day of salvation" (2 Cor 6:2).

4

———— ⊕ ————

CONTENTS FRAGILE AND WOUNDED:
PLEASE HANDLE WITH CARE!

THE prophet Isaiah proclaims the coming of a Servant of the Lord, who "shall bring forth justice to the nations, not crying out, not shouting, not making his voice heard in the street. A bruised reed he shall not break, and a smoldering wick he shall not quench, until he establishes justice on the earth" (Is 42:1-4). We Christians know that Christ fulfilled this prophecy as the true Suffering Servant, enduring human frailty to draw us into God's own life and taking on our sins through His suffering and death. And yet what do we make of the "bruised reed" and the "smoldering wick"? Are we not all bruised reeds whose courage is easily broken by the turbulent storms of daily life? Are we not all smoldering wicks whose light of love is easily quenched by neglect, slights, or harsh treatment?

≈

As I began this article, I noticed how the readings for the week after the Epiphany—the last week of Christmas on some years—proclaim the Messiah's coming to us in humility and weakness to manifest His love for us in our frailty. These readings flesh out the theme of Epiphany by emphasizing that in Jesus Christ God manifests Himself to us *not* in a majestic, overpowering way but in words and deeds of tender compassion. We see our Savior bringing about the Kingdom as He cured "all who were sick with various diseases and racked with pain" (Mt 4:24). Jesus pitied the vast crowd that lacked both food and good shepherds; so He taught them at great length and multiplied loaves and fishes for them (Mt 6:34-44). Our Lord walked on turbulent waters toward His fearful disciples and assured them, "Do not be afraid" (Mk 6:50).

In a show of humanly scandalous love, Jesus violated Jewish standards of cleanness as He "stretched out His hand" to touch a man full of leprosy and healed him (Lk 5:13). Furthermore, the readings from 1 John repeatedly enjoin us to love our brothers and sisters in the same tender, compassionate way: "Whoever does not love a brother whom he has seen cannot love [the] God he has not seen. This is the commandment we have from Him: whoever loves God must also love his brother" (1 Jn 4:20-21). Looking ahead to the season of Lent, we are invited to enter into this self-emptying love more deeply as we grow in awareness of our own brokenness and the burning need for salvation in Christ that we share with the rest of humanity.

෨

I once discovered that I had a case of athlete's foot, which was something new to me. One morning, as I delicately applied the ointment that a nurse had given me, I realized what a powerful lesson this slight ailment could teach. First of all, I had felt an itch for months without taking much notice or seeking treatment. How often do we pass our days without recognizing the wounds we carry about until some special situation reveals a deep hurt from the past? Secondly, I realized how carefully I had to apply the salve and to rub it in gently without worsening the wound. (One time, in fact, I hastily rubbed too hard and broke it open.) How much more carefully must we deal with the wounds in other people! If we are to be healers in the name of Christ, then we must apply the salve of Christ's love faithfully but gently, lest wounds break open at inopportune times and cause undue consternation. Thirdly, at one point I thought the infection was healed, and I stopped the treatment; but then I saw that the problem had not gone away. Just so, our emotional and spiritual wounds often linger for years, and sometimes for life. (What a good opportunity to keep acknowledging our frailty and welcoming the Lord's healing balm!) If, then, we know that we must treat bodily wounds so caringly and gingerly, how much more must we respect the fragile, wounded "contents" of our brothers and sisters, all of whom need Christ's gentle healing love! I suspect that we too often rub too hard in efforts to apply our *own* medicine to others' ailments instead of administering the "ointment of encouragement"[1] of our Suffering Servant, who never seeks to break what is bruised or quench what is smoldering.

∽

The *Rule* of Saint Benedict is written for a community of wounded persons. At the end of a series of precepts for dealing with wayward brothers, the abbot is enjoined to "realize that he has undertaken care of the sick, not tyranny over the healthy."[2] Therefore, "he is to imitate the loving example of the Good Shepherd."[3] Those who do not readily mend their faulty ways are to be given every possible opportunity to reform; at a certain point special communal prayers are to be said "so that the Lord, who can do all things, may bring about the health of the sick brother."[4] Monks who leave the monastery are to be given three chances to return again.[5] The cellarer and those who help him are to give out items in a gentle, respectful way so as not to lead "little ones" astray and are not to cause anyone to be "disquieted or distressed in the house of God."[6] The list of situations that allow for human frailty and summon monks not to take advantage of that frailty could go on and on. Especially striking is the passage summoning the abbot to show great tenderness and mercy. He "should always let mercy triumph over judgment (from Jas 2:13) so that he too may win mercy. He must hate faults but love the brothers. When he must punish them, he should use prudence and avoid extremes; otherwise, by rubbing too hard to remove the rust, he may break the vessel. He

---

1	RB 28:3
2	RB 27:6
3	RB 27:6
4	RB 28:5
5	RB 29
6	RB 31:19

is to distrust his own frailty and remember not to crush the bruised reed (from Is 42:3)."[7]

&

Carrying out this task of care-filled handling of our wounded sisters and brothers will surely point out our own radical need for God's grace. Over the years most of us have accumulated an array of prejudices, dislikes, and self-righteous norms that make it impossible to love certain people on a human level. However, "with God all things are possible" (Mk 10:27), and we must welcome our Savior to convince us of this truth and to do His work in us again and again. One key dimension of Saint Benedict's injunction that we "keep careful watch over all you do" and be "aware that God's gaze is upon you"[8] is to become adept at catching our mindless, judgmental thoughts and "dash[ing] them against Christ"[9] as soon as we notice them. Then, with Christ's transforming love, we can learn to see those around us as fragile, wounded creatures in urgent need of Christ's healing love and to see ourselves as potential instruments of that love. In fact, we can learn that those who annoy us most probably reveal to us negative traits that we hate in ourselves. Such people are not our enemies but fellow pilgrims who share our fragility and wounds and who can help to open us to the floodgates of Christ's love. When we learn to throw a glance of love at such people in place of arrows of judgment, then we are indeed letting Our Lord cast a glance of love at ourselves. Here there is a "multiplication of loaves"! With such a reformed vision of other people, we can proceed to handle others gently not only in our minds but also in our speech and action. When someone passes us in the hall, we can ready ourselves to share the other's burden if he or she shows any sign of revealing a personal problem. When people make impossible demands of us, we can give them back something more precious than whatever they request—a loving smile, a token of love, a reassurance that Christ will fill their neediness. When someone rebuffs or avoids us, then we can take on the role of the prodigal

---

7   RB 64:10-13
8   RB 4:48-49
9   RB 4:50

son's father and spare no effort to wait attentively for any sign of reconciliation. In all these ways, we can practice loving those whom we do not particularly like. We can become the healing balm of our Savior's love for those whose wounds have kept love away from them. We can boldly stretch ourselves out to touch those afflicted by the leprosy of self-hatred.

ℰ↷

In all these practices, of course, we need to be supported by lives of intensive prayer. In prayerful reflection on our own lives, we come to face our own fragility in the safety net of God's limitless mercy. In our *lectio divina* on interactions with others, we are confronted by our lamentable lack of compassionate concern. In our silence before the Lord, we come to know how precious we are in His eyes and how marvelously He uses even our weaknesses to carry out His work of healing wounded souls. Despite our own feebleness, we shall receive Christ's power to "strengthen the hands that are feeble, make firm the knees that are weak, [and] say to those whose hearts are frightened: Be strong, fear not!" (Is 35:3-4). May we daily welcome the grace to place healing salve on bruised reeds and to rekindle with the light of hope the smoldering wicks that we so often encounter in our fragile brothers and sisters!

5

ROADBLOCKS IN LIFE:
OCCASIONS FOR DEATH AND NEW LIFE

I have the strength for everything through him who empowers me.[1]

A T certain times of our lives we face major roadblocks, obstacles that leave us feeling devastated, helpless, empty, or generally unable to cope with life. Death, separation, serious illness, failure, financial losses, or the loss of work can also challenge our faith in the God who permits such crosses. Besides such gigantic roadblocks there are the daily frustrations, inconveniences, interruptions, and embarrassments that can render us chronically irritated, anxious, or fretfully dissatisfied with others or ourselves. In most cases we cannot control the circumstances that block our chosen path; hence the genuine frustration. However, we do have a choice as to how we deal with our frustration. Do we fret and fume, rant and rage, murmur and grumble; or do we clothe ourselves with faith, surrender ourselves, abandon ourselves, and offer ourselves eagerly, faithfully, and even joyfully to the Lord who makes all things new in His love?

❧

Not long ago, I confronted a very physical roadblock that stimulated me to reflect on roadblocks in general. As I set out on a one-day

---

1   Phil. 4:13

trip to attend a funeral 110 miles away, I experienced several obstacles that led me to wonder whether the Lord wanted me to go or not. First, I discovered that the assigned car had been reserved for the wrong day. After that problem was resolved at the last minute, there arose a difficulty concerning a hard-to-reach gas pedal. After a pillow marvelously appeared to remove that obstacle, I came to a construction zone, where the road ended without any sign for a detour. Fortunately, I noticed a nearby road crew, who gave me alternate directions for reaching my destination. Thanks be to God! Since I had five more hours of driving to reflect on these upsetting incidents, I realized that God's saving love had helped me to overcome each obstacle and to arrive where He apparently wanted me to be. Furthermore, since it was the Feast of the Guardian Angels, the patrons of our Benedictine Congregation, it occurred to me that *my* angel had indeed rescued me from very real adversities—and, more importantly, kept tugging at me to help me let go of fretting, murmuring, and every form of inner and outer anxiety. (Also, the words of a very powerful morning-Mass homily on the superfluity of God's providential love, as manifested in part by angels doing the work of Christ, God's true "Angel," made the experience of salvation all the more vivid for me.) I realized that it is not only amid concrete inconveniences and frustrations that God and His angels minister to us in powerful ways; it is to the very core of the wounded, self-centered, unredeemed dimensions of our beings that Christ *continually* ministers with His healing love; He uses *all* circumstances to encourage us to die to self, to be converted in His love, and to welcome the new redeemed life that thirsts even more for the fullness of salvation.

✧

The *Rule* of Saint Benedict offers us very relevant advice for responding to the roadblocks of life. Although life in the monastery is to be one of "peace" insofar as all seek to live in the peace of Christ, Saint Benedict realistically knew that a multitude of disturbances would daily challenge that peace; and he also knew that each incident of turmoil provided a precious opportunity from God for personal conversion. On the one hand, the *Rule* sounds a bit severe in urging us to bear with hardships without seeking escape. In *RB* 58 a candidate to monastic life is not to be granted an easy entry but is to be kept knocking at the door for four or five days; only if he bears patiently "his harsh treatment and difficulty of entry" and persists in requesting admission is he to be allowed to stay in the guest quarters.[2] In the Prologue, speaking of the strictness required "to amend faults and to safeguard love," Saint Benedict exhorts us, "Do not be daunted immediately by fear and run away from the road that leads to salvation."[3] Also, the often-quoted fourth step of humility commands the monk to embrace suffering quietly when obedience is required "under difficult, unfavorable, or even unjust conditions," and to endure all sorts of obstacles with faith, "without weakening or seeking escape."[4] Faith tells us, "we overcome because of Him who so greatly loved us."[5]

On the other hand, the *Rule* admonishes us *not* to place roadblocks in the way of others. In establishing "a school for the Lord's service," Saint Benedict hoped that his regulations would not deliberately generate anything harsh or burdensome.[6] The abbot must "use every skill of a wise physician" to support a wavering brother and arrange to "console him lest he be overwhelmed by excessive sorrow."[7] The cellarer is obliged to provide food "without any pride or delay," so that the brothers may not be led astray, and he is to give out items at the proper times "so that no one may be disquieted or distressed in the house of God."[8] The distribution of material goods is to be made according to individuals' genuine needs so that "all the members will be at peace."[9] Those whose weakness renders their kitchen duty difficult should be given help "so that they may serve without distress."[10]

---

2   RB 58:3-4
3   RB Prologue:47-48
4   RB 7:35-36
5   RB 7:39, quoting Rom 8:37
6   RB Prologue:46
7   RB 27:2-3
8   RB 31:16, 18-19
9   RB 34:1-5
10   RB 35:3

Time and again Saint Benedict stipulates that help should be given where it is needed so that unnecessary hardship might be avoided.[11]

℘

How, then, are we as Christians to face the roadblocks of life? Of course, first of all we should not *choose* to set up roadblocks—or any forms of suffering—in our paths; there are plenty that occur naturally every day as we strive to live in selfless love! In faith, however, we can state with certainty that every roadblock that does occur provides an opportunity for death to self and for conversion to a deeper trust in God. Our God of love surely does not manipulate circumstances to place extra burdens on us to test our faith; Jesus clearly showed and taught that God, our loving Father, does all He can to relieve our suffering. And yet, in another sense, God does "give us crosses to carry" insofar as He uses the sufferings of life to keep us turning to Him; the roadblocks, in particular, help us to seek out His *better* directions, those that will purify us from sinful patterns and gain us fuller salvation in Christ. As the Letter to the Hebrews urges us, "Endure your trials as 'discipline'; God treats you as sons. For what 'son' is there whom the father does not discipline...? We have had our earthly fathers to discipline us, and we respected them. Should we not [then] submit all the more to the Father of spirits and live?" (Heb 12:7-9). The discipline comes so that we might *live*. I know, for my part, that I *need* daily roadblocks to keep me from complacency, from addiction to my chosen schedule, from over-fascination with my work, from self-imposed isolation, and from obliviousness to the real needs of people around me. I must over and over learn that every hardship conceals a precious treasure from God, a call to let go of my illusory strength, to stop murmuring, to welcome His saving love, to put on a new heart and mind, and to *keep* relying on God, in Whom I have strength for everything that *He* wants me to do. Indeed, this is Good News, even if it often feels painful!

Thus, for all of us, to face daily roadblocks with faith, we must take care not to pamper ourselves by living in the illusion that "this

---

11   RB 31:17, 21:1, 36:10, 47:1, 53:1 & 20, 65:14-15

can't be!" or to pity ourselves or to seek pity from others. Another means of escape that I have sought is to think smugly, "This can't happen again!" Such a thought involves a phony consolation since, of course, something that seems far worse *can* and *might* happen! If I struggle to live mindfully, I shall believe that God is right here with me at the roadblock. He may lift the obstacle, as in the case of a healing; He may redirect me around the roadblock; or He may keep me stuck at the roadblock, so that I must die to my plans—or perhaps even die physically—and surrender myself fully to Him. In any case, the roadblock is an opportunity to die to self and rise with Christ, to suffer with Him so as to live with Him, to be converted in His love. When *I* cannot find a way, then *God* will show me the way. Despite my jittery feelings, I must learn to proclaim inwardly, "How wonderful that the Lord has come to redirect my ways! How I need this conversion, this renewal, this new life that comes through death!"

At the same time, roadblocks (especially when we experience them as arising from others' thoughtlessness or malice) teach us not to place obstacles in the paths of others and not to give them cause to lose heart. My success, my convenience, my sense of fulfillment must give way to the peace and salvation of other people. Quoting *Gaudium et spes*, the *Catechism* instructs us that "the order of things [and *my* sense of order] must be subordinate to the order of persons, and not the other way around" (# 1912). Building up others in love, in Christ, must be my first priority. Therefore, I must refrain from judgment or suspicion when others impose on me through their physical, moral, or emotional weaknesses; very often they are really doing the best they can. If I am able to live more simply than others, I must thank God and not nurture pride, envy, or anxiety for more; perhaps I should seek to live even more simply and thus try to be of greater assistance to the poor. If someone's language or manners cause me distress, I should thank the Lord for the opportunity to bear lovingly with someone very different from me. In some situations, I may be called upon to correct someone with gentleness, humility, and (always) love; but even then I must be careful not to cause the other unnecessary stress or anxiety, and I must be discerning enough to purify my motives of pride, vengeance, power, and personal convenience. The genuine good of the other, in the way directed by God, must always be my primary motive.

Yes, the roadblocks of life are meant by our loving God to redirect our paths to conform to His loving will for us. Let us also realize that almost every day far more situations go right than go wrong; our God is so indulgent as not to let too many roadblocks sap our hope! Through roadblocks we learn not to make plans without consulting our all-wise God. We learn to surrender our lives more and more to Him. We learn to rejoice in the daily struggle for personal conversion, for death to selfish ways, for a cheerful shouldering of our crosses, and for reliance on God's strength. Thus I become strong with Christ's strength of love rather than my illusory sense of control. As we daily face the small or large roadblocks of life, let us utter with Saint Paul, "I am content with weakness, insults, hardships, persecutions, and constraints, for the sake of Christ; for when I am weak, then I am strong" (2 Cor 12:10).

6

DRYNESS IN PRAYER:
PART OF THE NARROW ROAD
THAT LEADS TO SALVATION

ALL those who have made a sincere commitment to pray regularly know that prayer often doesn't go right. We say that such prayer is *dry*—unsatisfying, distracted, seemingly unanswered by God or not reaching God. Perhaps *dry* is too mild a term. People experiencing dryness in prayer might consider their prayer wildly distracted, full of miseries, or spoiled by worries and fears. In sum, the prayer somehow doesn't go the way we would like it to go, especially in our thoughts, feelings, and attention to God, and we may be tempted to discouragement, doubts about God's love for us, or fears that we are seriously displeasing God. In particular, if we are experiencing difficulties in life outside of prayer, we may reason, "At least, I should be getting some consolation from God in my prayer. Something must really be wrong in my life if I can't even pray well!"

Desolation, or spiritual darkness, is a more technical term for dryness in the spiritual life. Over the centuries spiritual masters have delved deeply into the theology and spirituality of consolations and desolations, and one can benefit greatly from the fruits of their meditations. One of my favorite books on the struggles of prayer life is

The Spiritual Letters of Dom John Chapman, O.S.B.,[1] and I strongly recommend it to Oblates. Abbot John Chapman of Downside Abbey, England, was gifted in advising people having problems with prayer. Another excellent resource is *When the Well Runs Dry*, by Father Thomas Green, S.J.[2]

What, then, do spiritual masters tell us about desolations? In some cases, we may be responsible for them. First, if there is serious immoral behavior in our lives, then we are likely to find prayer unsatisfying (if we try to pray at all) because God must use desolations to wake us up to correct the disorder in our lives. Secondly, we may not be praying enough, and we have simply not developed sufficient taste for prayer; and as a result, God, as it were, reproaches us through the dryness to get us to devote more time and attention to our prayer. If we do so, we are likely to begin enjoying the sweetness of God's love. Thirdly, it might be that in using time for prayer we are neglecting an urgent duty that we should be performing, such as reconciliation with someone or hospitality to someone who has arrived unexpectedly. Only after we have done our duty of love can we find peace in encountering the God of love in prayer.

Nonetheless, even when there is no serious neglect on our part, we still do experience dryness in prayer—perhaps even for days, months, or years. How can we explain such dissatisfying prayer when we are really doing our best to be good disciples of Christ? The following are just a few bits of traditional wisdom that may be of help:

(1) Life itself is full of dryness and trials; so why should we expect our prayer to be sweet and unproblematic?

(2) The problems of life naturally overflow into prayer since prayer is an integral part of life, and not a separate, idyllic world to which we flee to escape life.

(3) A physical or emotional condition may be hindering our attentiveness at prayer. Perhaps we have just eaten a heavy meal or have slept poorly the night before or are suffering allergy symptoms.

---

1   London: Sheed and Ward, 1946.
2   Ave Maria Press, 1979.

(4) Our physical environment may not be conducive to prayer. Perhaps some noise that is not under our control keeps us from settling down into an inner calm.

(5) Perhaps we are too intent on seeking consolation in prayer, and God is telling us to learn to "love the God of consolations more than the consolations of God." This is a widespread phenomenon, and I myself must learn this lesson over and over again!

(6) God may be drawing us out of one type of prayer and into another, such as a quieter, more contemplative approach.

What is important in each of the above situations is that God is using the desolation to draw us closer to Him. He is telling us that, despite our best of intentions, we are not in control of our prayer and we must learn to trust more in Him. Rather than let the dryness discourage us, we should accept our prayer and ourselves as we are, and then just keep praying as best we can. Our prayer is none the worse when it is dry. In fact, to think that we should be doing "better" can be a subtle form of pride. To judge that my prayer is not acceptable to God when God Himself is ready to accept whatever I have to offer with good intention is to be more exacting than the Lord who loves me as I am. Therefore, we can, in a sense, be consoled in the midst of our desolation by realizing, in faith, that God is with us despite our feelings and is helping us to engage in battle against prideful despondency, which the Devil can use to get us to give up altogether. We must know that God is telling us, "Do not lose hope! I have not abandoned you! Your darkness is a share in My Son's Cross, and through it you can grow in trust and love."

∽

Anyone who thinks that monks are accustomed to prayer that is always full of blissful consolations is very much mistaken. My prayer, both in private and in community, is far more often than not undramatic, frustrating, or even anguishing. When, for example, I am sitting at my *lectio divina*, I am sometimes surprised by a strong feeling of fear, anger, or resentment that arose from some event of the previous day. In such a case, I have come to believe that the feelings and the surrounding events come to my consciousness for a good reason. Sometimes I think the Lord wants me to deal with the situation directly by meditating on the specific details in light of His Word. At other times, I think He wants me to acknowledge the disturbing thought or feeling, to cast it into His hands, and then to put it aside so that I can deal with it later. In either case, I am regularly amazed how the negative feelings have dissipated. Surely, the Lord uses such disruptions of my *lectio* to make me aware of my vulnerability, to heal some of my wounds, to reconcile me to others, and to draw me close to Him in my weakness. Yes, prayer does and should make us more and more aware of our weaknesses.

&

It is often said that Saint Benedict wrote a rule for a monastery in which things are always going wrong. There is much truth in that generalization. Although the *Rule* says nothing specifically about desolation in prayer, there is much practical wisdom that can be applied to struggles in prayer. Evil promptings are likely to tempt the monk, both inside and out of prayer; when they come, he is urged to fling them "far from the sight of his heart... and [to dash] them against Christ."[3] Also, sorrow for sins is a necessary part of daily prayer,[4] and the tears and sighs that come with the prayer of repentance are not likely to be altogether consoling. The precept to pray for one's enemies[5] reminds the monk to deal with tensions with others, particularly in prayer; such prayer itself is likely to be strained and tense until the conflict is resolved. Having sinful thoughts and base desires, even during prayer,[6] can be part of the monk's growth in humility. In community prayer the task of getting minds in harmony with voices[7] is often likely to be a difficult struggle. Furthermore, the *Rule* honestly admits that monks (and many others!) may prefer sleep or idle talk to praying the Divine Office[8] and that monks will sometimes be

---

3   RB Prologue:28
4   RB 4:57-58
5   RB 4:72
6   RB 7:18, 24, 44
7   RB 19:7
8   RB 22:8, 43:8, 48:17-20

tardy in arriving to communal prayer.[9] Perhaps a monk's experience of dryness has caused him some loss of taste for prayer. Benedict's approach is to help the monk to keep praying anyway and thus to face the dryness head-on. In one part of the *Rule*,[10] Benedict implies that on a journey one may find it difficult to pray; but he insists that we should pray anyway, and do the best we can. Elsewhere he brings up the situation of another's noise and insensitivity that may upset a monk's prayer[11]; although Benedict legislates to eliminate the disturbance, it is also true that the monk trying to pray quietly may have to cope charitably with the noise and persevere in prayer amidst non-ideal conditions. Finally, I sometimes wonder whether Saint Benedict and the other monastic fathers called for such long hours of common prayer and *lectio divina* partly in order to force the monk to face darkness in prayer. (When one goes to Office eight times a day and meditates on the Word for two to three hours, one almost has to feel something other than uninterrupted consolation!) Perhaps this forced desolation really helped monks to abandon their sense of self-sufficiency and to live in deeper surrender to God and trust in His mercy.

∾

How are *we* to deal with dryness in prayer? In a nutshell, desolation always provides an opportunity for reform of our lives and our attitudes, for deeper trust in God, and for perseverance in undesirable circumstances, both inside prayer and outside of prayer. God is never discouraging us from coming to Him. He always has a lesson to teach us. What are some of the lessons we can learn?

(1) Prayer is not better because we feel good about it or have sweet thoughts of God. It is good because we are committed to prayer and are responding to God's call to pray. He is there whether we feel His presence or not. As Abbot John Chapman reminds us, "The will to pray is prayer."

---

9   RB 43:4-6
10   RB 50:4
11   RB 52:3-5

(2) Our "sweet" experiences at prayer are no indication of our closeness to God. They can delude us into self-satisfaction. In fact, the Devil can use consolations to deceive grave sinners that they are really pleasing God!

(3) Prayer, like every good thing, is more God's gift than our own doing. Yes, we need to dispose ourselves as best we can; but then it is really the Holy Spirit within us who prays (Rom 8:26), often accompanying us in our groanings, or perhaps groaning with us.

(4) Trying to control our prayer or to evaluate our prayer, especially during prayer, is generally futile. We can best evaluate and adjust our input to prayer outside times of prayer, especially with the help of an experienced director.

(5) Dryness can keep us humble and help us to cope with life. For those who love God, "all things work for good" (Rom 8:28), including desolation in prayer. We need to be grateful for all non-deliberate desolation. God gives us strength to persevere in prayer and to persevere in the dark moments of everyday life. They are all part of the Christian mystery.

(6) "Poor" prayer reminds us that we are, in fact, always poor before God! Rather than crave the riches of satisfying experiences (which is rather selfish), we need to accept the riches of God's grace amidst our poverty.

(7) When disturbances abound, we need to let our attention depart from them gently and not get angry at them or at ourselves; otherwise we are giving too much attention to ourselves instead of God. We must refocus on Christ or the subject of our meditation, even if we must do so thousands of times.

(8) We must simply do the best we can and stop worrying. God is with us; so why need we fear? In Christ, God has opened the way for us to communicate freely with Him as our loving Father, whether we feel good about it or not. What a gift!

(9) Abbot John Chapman tells us, "Pray as you can, and don't try to pray as you cannot." In other words, stop attempting to pray in ways that just don't work for you. Dryness sometimes tells us to stop clinging to our preconceived notion of how we should be praying.

Finally, it is important to know that when we feel we are not pray-ing well, we can and should offer our poor, distracted groanings to God in union with Christ in His Passion. When we truly want to pray "well" but feel that our prayer is sorely lacking, then we are undergoing a form of suffering, which is just one more instance of the many sufferings that we endure outside of prayer. United with Christ's suffering, the suffering that we bear in prayer as cheerfully as possible is part of the narrow road that leads to salvation; despite our regrettable feelings of God's remoteness, such prayer is indeed very pleasing to God, probably much more so than the self-satisfy-ing prayer that seems to assure us of our self-achieved status in the spiritual life. Cheerful acceptance of our dry prayer is just where God wants us to be!

℘

Both in consolation and in desolation God is calling us to a deeper, richer life in the love of Christ. God uses desolations in prayer, like all sufferings in life, to prune away our bad habits, self-sufficiency, and illusions about prayer, about ourselves, about God, and about life in general. To have consistently lofty thoughts and feelings during prayer would tempt us to identify God with those good experiences, whereas He is far beyond them, and might lead us to cling to such paltry satisfactions, whereas God is urging us to transcend them. If we are somehow responsible for the desolation, then we need to re-form the disorder in our lives and then get on with the prayer. If we are not responsible for the desolation, then we must simply persevere the best we can with the faith-knowledge that desolation is no indica-tion of God's displeasure. In all cases of our sincere prayer, the Lord embraces us and seeks to reach lovingly into every corner of our lives. Our task is to keep praying amidst all the dryness and "never [to] lose hope in God's mercy."[12] This is the narrow road that leads to salvation and total immersion in Christ!

---

12   RB 4:74

7

∞

STABILITY:
FAITHFULNESS IN LITTLE THINGS

T various moments of our lives we may feel moved to do *great things* for the Lord, who has loved us so overwhelmingly. After all, has He not done great things for *us* (Lk 1:49)? Should we not have opportunities to convert lost souls, to give great witness, to perform great cures, to raise precocious children, to organize great works of mercy, to write great music, or at least to pray powerful prayers with dramatic effects? If at one time we ever cherished such great hopes and then found our dreams unfulfilled, then perhaps we settled into lives of mild despair, indifference, or mindlessness; or perhaps we fell into the habit of rushing to do many things, as if to make up for the inability to do a few great things. However, a bit of reflection on Scripture and the Church's teaching reveals that our God also does *little things* for us and does them faithfully, carefully, and lovingly. Our heavenly Father "makes His sun rise on the bad and the good, and causes rain to fall on the just and the unjust" (Mt 5:45). He feeds the birds in the sky (Mt 6:26), "clothes the grass of the field" (Mt 6:30), and has counted every hair on our heads (Lk 12:7). Should not we, then, as the Father's children and as disciples of Jesus (who as true Son was also attentive to such little things as lifting up people by the hand after He had healed them), take special heed of the little things that occupy the bulk of our waking hours? Has not God Himself instructed us, "Whether you eat or drink, or whatever you do, do everything for the glory of God" (1 Cor 10:31)?

❧

I sometimes stand in awe of the little things ingrained in my memory which still influence my life and motivate me to thank God for the people whose loving attentiveness to detail have drawn my heart closer to the God who is ever mindful of me. When I was in college, a jovial barber on campus noticed a callous under my chin and urged me to use a silk handkerchief when I played the violin. (I did begin to use a handkerchief as a result of his kind insistence, and still do.) When I made my first vocation visit to Saint Vincent, a monk paused periodically during a long walk with me to pick up litter in our path; that image of good stewardship later stuck in my memory and influenced me to seek admission to the monastic community here. As a novice, I occasionally worked in a lab with a monk who would wash his hands slowly and carefully with a minimal amount of water. I once learned that he was deliberately trying to conserve water and to be mindful of the other people with whom we share this precious resource. All of these little incidents, and many more, remind me how important it is to do ordinary things with focus, mindfulness of God, and love. Our gentle attention to the details of everyday life and our struggle not to let our prideful minds wander to other matters reflect God's own faithfulness, enflesh our promise of stability, and can lead others to greater mindfulness of God.

❧

Our commitment to be *stable* (i.e., faithfully persevering at the task of the moment, however humble or trying) meets with much resistance in modern society. Our culture teaches us to hurry, to impress other people, and to earn lots of money, even if we do our jobs carelessly. We are urged to care for quantity rather than quality and to flit from one project to another, like successive images on a television screen, according to our whimsical desires. Of course, there are times when we may *need* to work quickly, and perhaps even hastily, to respond to some emergency. However, if we have lapsed into the habit of always working hastily, then some examination of conscience may show that we are ignoring the very essence of our lives, in terms of relationships with God and with others, as we seek to "gain the whole world" (Lk 9:25). Furthermore, we may have to redo what we have done sloppily; we often end up having to pay for our mindlessness. When I begin to type hastily, I make typographical errors and forget that every tap of the finger is a gift of God. When I begin to turn pages of a book too quickly, I do damage to them and forget about others with whom I share this resource. When I tie my shoelaces unthinkingly, they readily become untied. Yes, when I become careless at the little tasks of life, I cause frustration to myself, detract from others' capacity to enjoy things, become less lovingly available to others, and lose a sense of reverence for God, who seeks to save me and draw me to Himself by the very "stubbornness" of things, which by their natures rebel when I treat them irreverently. Blessed be God for my shoelace which requires a double knot and, therefore, extra time and attention to be untied! When I seek to untie it hastily, the knot becomes even tighter. When I am faithful to the little task of untying it gently, then my very act of slowing down helps me to welcome God's grace and to surrender to Him in the *little thing* of untying knots.

❧

The aim of Benedictine prayer is to assist the monk to live his whole life in eager receptivity to God's will. He is to *become* a "living prayer." He is to live a life progressively dedicated to God and responsive to grace in every circumstance. The vow of stability limits the monk's outer "coming and goings" to render him more sensitive to the workings of grace here and now. Even more significantly, the vow is meant to cultivate stability in the heart, so that the monk may faithfully focus and refocus on Christ amidst life's undramatic demands. Thus every task becomes a sacred task. Early in the *Rule* we are urged, "Every time you begin a good work, you must pray to [God] most earnestly to bring it to perfection."[1] Of course, Saint Benedict is not referring to *our* standards of perfection, which can plunge us into a frenzy of perfectionist impulses, but rather to God's standards of doing everything for the love of Christ. Unlike the Sarabaites, who do

---

1   RB Prologue:4

"whatever strikes their fancy,"[2] and the Gyrovagues, who "are slaves to their own wills and gross appetites,"[3] the stable monk knows that "the love of Christ must come before all else."[4] The monk heeds the admonition, "Hour by hour keep careful watch over all you do, aware that God's gaze is upon you, wherever you may be."[5] The words "every time" and "wherever" are crucial. The monks even sleep clothed and girded so that they may always be ready for the sacred task of rising to the signal.[6] It is the abbot himself who keeps a list of tools and goods of the monastery[7] to remind the whole community that responsiveness to God requires the reverent use of all things. The act of blessing kitchen servers and the reader at meals stirs the monks to recognize the sacredness of cooking, washing, and serving at table, as well as of the very act of eating. In all such situations it falls upon the monk to be faithful in little things, for he is learning to "do everything in the name of the Lord Jesus" (Col 3:17), "so that in all things God may be glorified."[8]

❧

Since in following the spirit of the *Rule* Oblates make a promise of stability, they too have a sacred calling to be faithful in little things. How can we become more attuned and responsive to the call of God in the ordinary tasks of life? Perhaps it is a matter of learning to consecrate one activity after another. Perhaps it means bringing a sacred word from our *lectio* into some new task every so often until it becomes clear that this little piece of work is not mine to grasp but God's gift to be carried out gently and lovingly. Perhaps it involves catching myself every time I become hasty and careless, reproving myself gently but firmly,[9] and drawing myself to focus on Christ. Yes, Our Lord steps into the midst of my impulsiveness, longing to

---

2   RB 1:8
3   RB 1:11
4   RB 4:21
5   RB 4:48-49
6   RB 22:56
7   RB 3:23
8   1 Pt 4:11 & RB 57:9
9   cf. RB 32:4

redeem me! Little by little, my going to the barber, picking up of litter, untying of shoelaces, turning of pages, and talking with reverent attention to the person before me become sacred tasks. And they become sacred not just for my personal sanctification, but also for the good of those around me and indeed for the good of the whole Church. When I allow love to impel me[10] to do whatever I do in the ordinary duties of life, then I become a more generous self-offering to others as well as to God.

Even in the writing and the reading of this letter we can learn to focus on Christ, to be stable and rooted in Him, and to be faithful to doing our little tasks with love. Let us together be swept up in the sacredness of this present moment as we heed what we type, and as we heed what we read. In the word of 1 Peter 4:11, "Whoever serves, let it be with the strength that God supplies, so that in all things God may be glorified through Jesus Christ, to whom belongs glory and dominion forever and ever."

---

10   RB 5:10

8

BRINGING OTHERS JOY,
NOT SADNESS

IT was during Holy Week that I began to scribble down reflections for this essay. A central message of the Scripture readings and the liturgies of the Sacred Triduum is that Christ suffered and died for us out of love. He also rose for us out of love and the desire to share eternal life—divine life of immeasurable joy—with us. Christ ardently longs that we respond to His love with growing trust and love, limited though our capacity may be, and He wishes us not to sadden or scandalize one another but rather to encourage one another on our pilgrimage of faith with all its heavy burdens. Just as Christ died for all, the just and the unjust, the born and the unborn, the young and the old, the strong and the weak, the imprisoned and the free, so must our love be extended to all those whom Christ has redeemed by His blood. We must have reverence and respect for all human life; and, insofar as we can, we are to bring others spiritual joy rather than additional distress.

☙

I myself was once blessed with an experience of unexpected joy on a Good Friday as I held a crucifix for members of a small congregation to reverence. In an unusually moving way, I could sense the people's love for our crucified Lord as well as His love for each of them in their varied walks of life. Surely, He wants all of us to rejoice in His passionate love even as we mourn His terrible death. He suffered and died to redeem all human life, no matter how convincingly that life might be degraded by society. Every human life is precious to Him. He gave His life for each one of us.

Last January I experienced the preciousness of human life in another way that was new and unique for me. After years of thinking about attending the annual March for Life but never quite making it, I was finally moved by people and events (perhaps reflecting the Holy Spirit's initiatives) to make the commitment to go to Washington, DC. It was a sacrifice of time and energy, and that, of course, caused my timid, reluctant side to wonder what I was doing. However, my better self realized that the sacrifice was well worth making because, especially this year, the lives of the unborn and the elderly in this country may be threatened more than ever before by the encroachment of the *culture of death*. Among the highlights of my journey with Saint Vincent monks and seminarians were a vigil Mass in the National Shrine of the Immaculate Conception and a morning Mass in the Verizon Center. Both the basilica and the arena were filled to capacity, and overflow crowds had to be accommodated elsewhere. I felt honored before the morning Mass to be among the priests (perhaps hundreds of us) hearing the confessions of thousands of penitents for an hour and a half. That encouraging experience reminded me that those of us who strive to defend and promote the rights of vulnerable human beings must ourselves acknowledge our weakness and vulnerability and realize how easily we can sin against human life through anger, judgment, or failure to listen; we ourselves are in radical need of God's grace to bring us forgiveness and renewed strength. Still slaves to sinful tendencies, we need ongoing repentance to render us capable of fighting against the evil in our culture and of extending Christ's love unselfishly even to those who most repel us.

❦

The *Rule* of Saint Benedict, always reflecting the values of the Gospel, supports the dignity of those who are needy, frail, and vulnerable. Although Saint Benedict probably did not have to deal with unborn children or the problem of abortion, he did have to consider the welfare of those in the monastery (or its school or guest house) who were vulnerable because of old age, youth and inexperience, poor health, weariness from travel, or wayward tendencies. For all such people the *Rule* shows special consideration because of their individual needs and because of Christ's particular presence in them. Whereas Roman society fostered the institution of slavery, Saint Benedict puts monks who are ex-slaves on an equal footing with the freeborn; he stipulates, "A man born free is not to be given higher rank than a slave who becomes a monk, except for some other good reason."[1] Saint Benedict also insists, "Care of the sick must rank above and before all else, so that they may truly be served as Christ."[2] Furthermore, the "very weak" are even allowed to eat meat until they recover.[3] In sum, each person should be treated according to his weaknesses and genuine needs; each one must be embraced as a child of God. In this spirit the cellarer of the monastery should be "like a father to the whole community";[4] he should humbly offer those who request goods that are not available "a kind word in reply";[5] and he will respect his brothers' needs for nourishment by providing "the brothers their allotted amount of food without any pride or delay, lest they be led astray."[6] One who respects the dignity of all people and serves them with love also hastens them on the way to salvation.

Saint Benedict's precept about listening to younger members of the community is also part of the Christian call to reverence all human life. At community meetings the abbot is to call together the *whole* community, even the very young, because "the Lord often reveals what is better to the younger."[7] In today's world are not the unborn and the very young those to whom we must listen intently? Are they not crying out, "Look, we are truly alive human beings! We deserve dignity and legal protection to live our vocations in this life and to prepare for eternal life. Please do not treat us like mere blobs of inert tissue! Do not snuff out our God-given life!" Today scientific

---

1	RB 2:18
2	RB 36:1
3	RB 36:9
4	RB 31:2
5	RB 31:13
6	RB 31:16
7	RB 3:3

probes and videotapes of the unborn are verifying what believers have known all along: the unborn are fully and truly human beings; they deserve our respect and reverence.

Naturally, the *Rule* is pro-life because the Scriptures and the teachings of the Church have, from the beginning, proclaimed that all human life is sacred (even if that wonderful truth has often not been put into practice). Reflecting on Matthew 5:21-22 and Exodus 20:13 ("You shall not kill"), the *Catechism of the Catholic Church* asserts, "Human life is sacred because from its beginning it involves the creative action of God and it remains for ever in a special relationship with the Creator, who is its sole end. God alone is the Lord of life from its beginning until its end: no one can under any circumstance claim for himself the right directly to destroy an innocent human being."[8] Just as God tells the prophet Jeremiah, "Before I formed you in the womb I knew you" (Jer 1:5[†]) and just as the Psalmist reflects in amazement, "Nor was my frame unknown to you when I was being made in secret" (Ps 139:15[†]), so the *Catechism* teaches, "Human life must be respected and protected absolutely from the moment of conception"[9]. Likewise, "direct euthanasia... is morally unacceptable,"[10] and "an act or omission which, of itself or by intention, causes death in order to eliminate suffering constitutes a murder gravely contrary to the dignity of the human person and to the respect due to the living God, his Creator."[85] The *Catechism* goes on to condemn other ways of violating respect for human life: scandal, abuse of one's health, scientific research that does not promote the dignity of persons, disrespect for the dead, anger and hatred, and the destruction of human life in war.[11]

❧

How, then, are Oblates and monks today to show the reverence for human life that is taught in the Gospels and demanded by the *Rule*? It is a foregone conclusion that all of us must oppose abortion

---

8   #2258
9   #2270
10   #2277
11   #2284-2317

and euthanasia. Most of us will probably never have a major impact on our culture through legislation or court battles. We can, however, use our voting power and whatever other influence we have to combat one or both of these great evils. On a daily basis we are more likely to encounter other sorts of vulnerable people: the very young, the very old, the infirm, the unemployed, the wayward person, the unexpected guest, the annoying customer, or the person with disagreeable habits. Saint Benedict has much to say about our disposition toward such people. He tells us, "Great care and concern are to be shown in receiving poor people and pilgrims, because in them more particularly Christ is received."[12] Similarly, we are to "relieve the lot of the poor, clothe the naked, visit the sick, and bury the dead,"[13] and we are also to "go to help the troubled and console the sorrowing."[14] It may be very tempting at times to dismiss or put down people who make demands on us, but Saint Benedict insists that we, like the cellarer, are to offer others "a kind word in reply"[15] when we cannot meet their demands; we are also to strive not to impose on others "so that no one may be disquieted or distressed in the house of God."[16] Yes, our environment can become "the house of God" when we treat others around us with the reverence we owe to Christ. Is there not enough misery in the world without our adding to it? (We probably accidentally add to it in many ways.) Are we not called to give others some relief from their burdens so that a ray of sunshine from God may brighten them? Are we not called to take time to be with others in need and to listen to them "with the ear of [our] heart?"[17]

உ

Only in recent years have I heard the phrase "stealing someone's joy," which apparently means depriving others of their need for joy and hopefulness through negative, critical, bitter, or cynical attitudes, words, or behavior. Since Saint Paul commands us to "rejoice always"

12   RB 53:15
13   RB 4:14-17
14   RB 4:18-19
15   RB 31:13
16   RB 31:19
17   RB Prologue:1

(1 Thes 5:16[†]), are we not to help one another obey this precept? Since Saint Benedict urges us not to burden the sick or weak with unreasonable expectations,[18] are we not to strive to bring them a taste of joy instead of "overwhelming them or driving them away?"[19] It is most especially in *RB* 31 that Saint Benedict adjures a trusted official, the cellarer, and thus also us, who are all in some sense stewards and dispensers of goods, not to annoy others. He "should not annoy the brothers."[20] He must see that the brothers not "be led astray"[21] through his pridefulness or delay. He must "not reject [anyone] with disdain and cause him distress."[22] In *RB* 31:16, Saint Benedict quotes Saint Matthew's Gospel 18:6, "It would be better for anyone who leads astray one of these little ones who believe in me, to be drowned by a millstone around his neck." Later on, Christ again warns, "See that you never despise one of these little ones. I assure you, their angels in heaven constantly behold my heavenly Father's face" (Mt 18:10[†]). Who are these "little ones"? Are they not all of us insofar as we are weak, vulnerable, easily hurt, and often discouraged? Perhaps the "little ones" today are most especially the unborn, the elderly, the abused, the homeless, the sick who receive inadequate care, and those in prison. Of course, sometimes the wayward need to be corrected since love sometimes requires a firm "No," and once in a while you or I may be the one called to do the correction. However, we are called never deliberately to sadden or disdain or discourage anyone. Rather, we need to bring to others a modicum of Christian joy, which is in such short supply in our world. The joy that comes with knowing that we are lavishly loved by God and that we already possess that joy, insofar, as Christ has given Himself totally to us in His Passion and death and has raised us up with Him in His Resurrection and Ascension.

℘

18	RB 48:24-25
19	RB 48:24
20	RB 31:6
21	RB 31:16
22	RB 31:7

As during Easter Season, let us remember that the risen Christ comes to us in the least expected people and situations. He brings us peace and wants us to rejoice in Him (Jn 20:20[†]) and to show Him reverential love (Mt 28: 9, 17[†]). It is through our practice of self-denial in order to make room for others that we share in Christ's Passion, and it is in the deference and reverence we show to others that we honor Christ Himself (Eph 5:21[†]). Let us, with the grace of our risen Lord, learn to bear patiently with those who cause us pain "because serving them leads to a greater reward"[23]—the reward of eternal life and of a marvelous, joyful communion with Our Lord and all the saints that begins even in this life.

---

23   RB 36:5

9

DETACHMENT:
LEAVING EVERYTHING BEHIND
TO GAIN WHAT REALLY MATTERS

OUR materialistic world tempts us to acquire as many possessions and pleasures as we possibly can. Subtle but powerful
psychological appeals urge us to become attached to particular brands of food, clothes, cosmetics, pharmaceuticals, and cars
so that we may keep buying more and more, desiring more and more,
and thus having no time or energy to ponder the deeper meaning of
life. In contrast, Christ lovingly but sternly exhorts us, "Whoever
wishes to come after me must deny himself, take up his cross, and
follow me. For whoever wishes to save his life will lose it, but whoever loses his life for my sake will find it" (Mt 16:24-25). He likewise
warns us, "Everyone of you who does not renounce all his possessions
cannot be my disciple" (Lk 14:33). In Saint John's Gospel, Jesus summons us to detachment and renunciation in a more symbolic way:
"I say to you, unless a grain of wheat falls to the ground and dies, it
remains just a grain of wheat; but if it dies, it produces much fruit.
Whoever loves his life loses it, and whoever hates his life in this world
will preserve it for life eternal" (Jn 12:24-25).

❧

Christian detachment involves not only restraint on desires for
material goods; it also applies to attitudes toward intellectual and

spiritual goods. It must affect, for example, our approach to *lectio divina*; we must learn to accept even those words of Scripture that we find least appealing. In my personal cycle of readings for *lectio*, I recently turned to the Book of Numbers. Even in my better moments I was not especially eager to plow through lists of census figures and detailed specifications of the duties of Levitical clans. Nonetheless, I committed myself to struggle with all 36 chapters, with less time and energy, of course, devoted to the seemingly routine descriptions. As it turns out, I did find some gems amid the less attractive passages. When the twelve princes of Israel were preparing to make offerings to God to commemorate the consecration and dedication of the altar in the Dwelling, they apparently had intended to bring their offerings all on one day. However, "the Lord said to Moses, 'Let one prince a day present his offering for the dedication of the altar'" (Num 7:11). There follows a long list of apparently identical offerings made by each of the princes, beginning with Judah's (Num 7:12-88). Pondering this call to distribute the offerings over twelve days, I was reminded of our need to offer ourselves to God over and over; one or two self-offerings a day will not suffice. A morning offering alone (although it is an excellent practice) will not suffice. God asks of us, in Christ, to make continual offerings of praise and thanksgiving. The offering that we make in the morning must be repeated often, especially when the demands of the day tempt us to give in to discouragement or self-will. Again and again, perhaps many times each day, we are to detach ourselves from self-centered impulses and reattach ourselves to God's will as we can best understand it. Thus, in communion with Christ, we need regularly to rededicate ourselves as "living sacrifices of praise."[1]

∾

Detachment and death to self, being essential to all Christian life, are also prominent in Benedictine spirituality. Saint Benedict, knowing that we are creatures who tend to self-will, warns the monk against drifting away from God "through the sloth of disobedience";

---

1   Eucharistic prayer 4

only the "labor of obedience" will bring him back.[2] The disciple must repeatedly detach himself from old, comfortable behavioral patterns, such as vicious talk, deceit, injustice, slander, susceptibility to temptation, and self-satisfaction.[3] Recognizing that we can become complacent about our faults, Saint Benedict urges us to adopt "a little strictness in order to amend faults and to safeguard love."[4] The abbot, like any Christian, must continually detach himself from any attitudes and practices that keep him from Christ-like leadership. He is to avoid favoritism,[5] must shun "too great concern for the fleeting and temporal things of this world,"[6] and should regularly seek "the amendment of his own faults."[7] All the brothers are to keep from defending "their own views obstinately,"[8] from following their own hearts' selfish desires,[9] and from rashly deviating from the *Rule*.[10] Everyone is to be on guard against wrongful thoughts, which, as soon as they enter one's heart, are to be "dash[ed]... against Christ,"[11] who alone has the power to overcome them. Thus the basic thrust of spiritual detachment is to overcome and transcend self-will in its many forms. Acknowledging this, monks choose "to live in monasteries and to have an abbot over them."[12] The obedience that they offer must be "free from any grumbling or any reaction of unwillingness"[13] and "must be given gladly";[14] otherwise they are still fundamentally attached to their own wills. As an outward expression of inner detachment, a monk gladly rids himself of his possessions "without keeping back a single thing for himself,"[15] and his being stripped of possessions and of worldly clothes symbolizes his commitment to make

2   RB Prologue:2
3   RB Prologue:17, 26-29
4   RB Prologue:47
5   RB 2:16-22
6   RB 2:33
7   RB 2:40
8   RB 3:4
9   RB 3:8
10   RB 3:7
11   RB 4:50
12   RB 5:12
13   RB 5:14
14   RB 5:16
15   RB 58:24

himself a total self-gift to Christ; in fact, "from that day [of vows] he will not have even his own body at his disposal."[16] Because the monk belongs totally to God, any attachment that impedes this complete commitment must be left behind. In place of former attachments he gains an eternal dwelling with God, even in this life, and he finds the deep and lasting joy of "[preferring] nothing whatever to Christ."[17]

ᘒ

In his book *Strangers to the City*, Father Michael Casey, O.C.S.O. treats "dispossession" as a key monastic value. He reflects on dispossession in terms of the categories of material poverty, poverty of spirit, and the fragility of life. Referring to the trials of this life, he asserts:

> *It is eschatological hope that allows the monk to take present reverses less seriously and to hanker less intensely for the conveniences and gratifications that will last only for a time. This attitude derives not from negativity toward created reality itself, but from the recognition that when affections and desires become fixated at a level below the optimum, one's whole personhood is devalued and one's sensibility is debased... Monastic tradition is formed around a firm faith that as human beings we are intended for union with God. Nothing else can fully satisfy us. To allow ourselves to be diverted by the pursuit of temporal realities in such a way that our spiritual energies are diminished is ultimately self- diminishing. (p. 89)*

The occasion of ultimate dispossession is one's death, over which we have little or no control but in which we have a marvelous opportunity for total self-surrender to God. Of course, the better we practice surrendering ourselves during daily life, the better we are likely to do it at death and the less purgation we are likely to require. The critical role of death in our surrender to God may explain why Saint Benedict exhorts us, "Day by day remind yourself that you are

---

16   RB 58:25
17   RB 72:11

going to die."[18] A healthy, Christ-centered outlook on death can help
us to detach ourselves from relatively unimportant earthly concerns
and to embrace the values that lead to everlasting life, which is a matter of relationships with God and with others who are in communion
with Him. The death of a loved one can also reorient us to embrace
that which truly lasts.

As some of you know, my mother died rather unexpectedly. In
the days before her death, I had been planning to work intensively
on mail on the days following her death; instead I ended up being
deeply involved with meetings (in conjunction with my sister) with
a real-estate agent, an undertaker, and a lawyer; with efforts to clean
the house and search through files; with arrangements for the funeral
services; and with a rummaging through material things with some
discernment about how to dispose of them. The disorientation that
I experienced guided me to view all other projects in proper perspective and to cherish the lasting relationships with God and with fellow
human beings that fueled me to enter into a series of unexpected
tasks with relative peace. The marvelous kindness and generosity of
people almost naturally came to the forefront of my mind. Most especially, the arrival of eight monks for the funeral (450 miles from the
Archabbey) caused me to be overwhelmed with gratitude for God's
lavish love. What else matters, I realized, than that we hold on only
very lightly to our plans and the things of this world and that we use
all the gifts of God to hasten one another on to eternal life in Christ?
What else matters than that we do everything with love and, therefore, detach ourselves from every less worthy motive?

Regarding death, Father Michael Casey comments:

> [when we] *turn our attention to the certainty of death,* [we
> can see that] *I had better hurry up and get started on doing
> the things that I want to have done during my lifetime. For the
> night comes when no one can do any work. And so, whether we
> voluntarily anticipate death by self-dispossession or whether we
> cling tightly until the last moment, at the end we are all called to*

---

18   RB 4:47

detachment not only from material realities but from bodily in-
stincts and eventually from the body and from life itself. (p. 88)

༄

This coming Lent might be a propitious time to examine our attachments and to ask the Lord to help us to become more detached
so that we might have more room for our relationship with Him.
Are we too caught up in buying, spending, and frantic working? Are
we intent upon remaking other people according to our ideals? Are
we so invested in plans for the future that we would be inclined to
despair should they fall through? Are we over-concerned about our
appearance or about food, clothes, and furniture? Are we driven to
succeed at all costs in some realm of activity? As we examine where we
need most to be freed from such attachments, let us remember that
our baptism commits us daily to die to self and to rise with Christ.
Let us recall that Benedictine life requires an ongoing denial of selfish impulses so that we can recommit ourselves to *lectio*, the Divine
Office, acts of loving service, deeper personal involvement with others in community, and everything else that helps us to live in fuller
communion with Christ. (A retreat or day of recollection can also do
wonders to shake us loose of our attachments.) Like the monk who
is "stripped of everything of his own that he is wearing,"[19] let us ask
for the grace to "put to death, then, the parts of you that are earthly"
(Col 3:5) so that we may clothe ourselves "with kindness, humility,
meekness, and patience" (Col 3:12), "put on love" over all these other
virtues (Col 3:14), and "put on the Lord Jesus Christ, and make no
provision for the desires of the flesh" (Rom 13:14).

---

19   RB 58:26

10

---◯◯◯---

QUIETLY ENCOURAGING ONE ANOTHER: NURTURING FAITH AMID TRIALS

How much time and energy we spend trying to overcome suffering! Human remedies sometimes do bring us significant relief, and these can indeed be mediated gifts from God. In most cases, however, there is no lasting remedy despite all the powers of science and technology. In our pilgrimage of faith, we know that the ultimate consolation for our suffering comes from the Cross, whereby Christ compassionately unites us with Himself and shares our every suffering, and from the Resurrection, whereby Christ gives us victory over sin, death, and discouragement and offers us new life in communion with Him. One of the means given to us for our participation in this victory is mutual encouragement in the love of Christ.

❧

The word *encourage* is a powerful one. Since it comes from the Latin word for heart, *cor*, one could say that encourage means "strengthen the heart." In fact, we have the roughly equivalent word *hearten*. We also sometimes say, "Do not lose heart." Since in spirituality the heart is a person's core or deepest center, where he or she encounters God, encouragement in the Christian sense serves to strengthen faith and to nurture relationships with God, especially amid feelings of doubt and fear. Many psalms abound in words that encourage us to hope in God, who is all-reliable. Psalm 27 ends with the exhortation, "Wait for the Lord, take courage; be stouthearted, wait for the Lord."[1] Psalm 31 ends in much the same way. Psalm 59 includes the refrain, "My strength, your praise will I sing; you, God, are my fortress, my loving God."[2] The Lord orders Moses to "encourage and strengthen" his successor, Joshua, to carry out his mission to lead the Israelites into the Promised Land (Deut 3:28). The Lord is always encouraging people to have faith and to fulfill their vocation in life despite oppressive burdens and severe trials. At the same time God often works through human instruments to convey His encouragement. Saint Paul writes to the Corinthians, "Blessed be the God and Father of our Lord Jesus Christ, the Father of compassion and the God of all encouragement, who encourages us in our every affliction so that we may be able to encourage those who are in any affliction with the encouragement with which we ourselves are encouraged by God... If we are afflicted, it is for your encouragement and salvation; if we are encouraged it is for your encouragement, which enables you to endure the same sufferings that we suffer" (2 Cor 1:4,6). At the end of the letter, the Apostle likewise heartens his people, "Mend your ways, encourage one another" (2 Cor 13:11). When the Council of Jerusalem decided in favor of welcoming Gentiles into the Church and sent representatives to Antioch to announce the decision, the Bible records that "When it was read there was great delight at the encouragement it gave" (Acts 15:31[†]).

℘

Encouragement can come in unexpected ways. About once every two months I am assigned to celebrate Mass at a mental institution, where one readily witnesses profound sufferings stemming from the patients' physical, emotional, and relational disorders. To most of us these afflictions would seem unimaginably oppressive. During the prayers of the faithful the residents often add their own intercessions, and it is then that some of their heartfelt concerns are revealed. Also, some in the congregation have questions and comments during the time of the homily. On one Sunday in particular, the chapel was almost

---

1   Psalms 27:14
2   Psalms 59:18; cf. 59:10

unbearably hot, and there was no way of lowering the heat. I myself, wearing rather thick priestly vestments, was sorely tempted to murmur about the situation. However, the congregation, some of whom were also heavily dressed, seemed to bear the heat with remarkable patience. In fact, during my homily they made more comments than usual, and these dealt largely with heaven, hell, purgatory, and eternal life. After the struggle to preach in that overheated environment with all the interruptions, I realized what encouragement the Lord was giving me through the precious people in front of me. If they could focus their attention on spiritual matters amid such discomfort and all their other problems, could I not do likewise? Similarly, at the sign of peace and during the time of departure, I often see evidence of the patients' tender compassion for one another and their promises of prayers for one another; and then I must ask myself whether I cannot nurture the same Christ-centered disposition in myself even when I am enduring some far less severe trial.

eɔ

Mutual encouragement in the name of Christ is an essential element of Christian community. It is not just a way to make people feel happy but a God-given means of hastening disciples on their heavenward pilgrimage amid the discouragement that suffering can engender. Although the *Rule* of Saint Benedict uses the word *encourage* (*cohortari* in Latin) only twice, the spirit of mutual encouragement pervades the *Rule*. In the chapter on the monks' sleeping arrangements, the concluding verse states, "On arising for the Work of God, they will quietly encourage each other, for the sleepy like to make excuses."[3] This almost hidden sentence encapsulates much of the essence of cenobitic monastic life and Christian family life. We all grow "sleepy" and spiritually weary at times. We are all tempted to be lax in our prayer now and then. We all benefit from others' encouragement to overcome our spiritual tepidity and to recommit ourselves to be zealously faithful to prayer and works of sacrificial love. We regain spiritual courage from such gentle but firm reminders

---

3   RB 22:8

from others in family and community. Amid temptations to make excuses for not praying as well or as much as we should, we can benefit from quiet but persistent words of encouragement from spiritual directors, family members, and other fellow Christians to return to the narrow path of disciplined prayer. The *Rule* itself and the abbot as well need to "prompt us to a little strictness in order to amend faults and to safeguard love."[4] In particular, all superiors are to give encouragement by their good example since, as stated in the *Rule's* eighth step of humility, every monk is to look to "the example set by his superiors"[5] as a standard for his own behavior. Without some degree of rigorous discipline, we shall never make progress in overcoming sinful tendencies and welcoming God to expand our narrow hearts into the realm of generous, selfless love. At the same time, the establishment of norms must always be made out of love, genuine concern for people's spiritual growth, and particular compassion for people in their weaknesses, which must always be taken into account.

Mutual encouragement is opposed to nagging and angry criticism. Those who try to change others out of a sense of frustration are likely to make matters worse because of their lack of compassion. Encouragement ultimately comes from God, and God never violates our freedom or dignity. Thus the abbot is to lead and teach most especially by the way he lives; "he must point out to them all that is good and holy more by example than by words."[6] In correcting and punishing, the abbot must "avoid extremes; otherwise, by rubbing too hard to remove the rust, he may break the vessel"; he is to prune away faults "with prudence and love as he sees best for each individual" and is to "strive to be loved rather than feared."[7] Also, the abbot must not be "excitable, anxious, extreme, obstinate, jealous or oversuspicious";[8] such traits would tend to cause reactions of fear, mistrust, or disdain in others and thus hamper spiritual growth. The cautions that Saint Benedict voices regarding the abbot's call to be an

---

4   RB Prologue:47
5   RB 7:55
6   RB 2:12
7   RB 64:12, 14, 15
8   RB 64:16

instrument of encouragement apply readily to other authorities, such as parents, teachers, pastors, and spiritual directors.

Our need for mutual encouragement and mutual obedience is addressed by Father Michael Casey, O.C.S.O., in the chapter entitled "Mutuality" in his book *Strangers to the City*.[9] He states:

> *A monk committed to the practice of mutual obedience is one who has come to the realization that he could be instructed and formed by many members of the community whose monastic experience was broader and deeper than his own. If he remains alert, each day will bring hundreds of opportunities in which he can say 'yes' to God and 'no' to self-will.* (p. 106)

The self-denial that we exercise in family and community not only nurtures Christ's love among us, but it also provides edification and encouragement to others who are eager to be formed in Christ. Father Michael further comments:

> *True community is built on self-denial... If I think of others only when I feel like it, then my service is no more than an arcane form of self-pleasuring. If my concern is limited to a select few, then it is beginning to look like a form of patronage, and we know how strongly Benedict rejected that.[10] My part in creating a climate of mutuality is to hold back on self-assertion so as to leave room for others. I must be constantly inviting others to flow into the common space, welcoming them, affirming them, even though this has to be done at the price of not asserting my own rights.* (pp. 110-111)

The author later continues:

> *Everyone is defective in something. As a result we need one another, and we need to recognize, appreciate, and encourage the*

---

9   Paraclete Press. Brewster, MA: 2005.

10   RB 69:1-4

different giftedness of others as a means of ensuring the common progress that provides a matrix for my own growth (p. 112)

❧

During the Easter Season the words of Scripture offer us special encouragement in the exhortations of the risen Lord and of the apostles, once the Twelve (with Judas replaced by Matthias) have been filled with the Holy Spirit. Immediately after the Resurrection, when the disciples are weak in faith and fearful, the risen Christ again and again wishes them peace (Mt 28:9; Jn 20:19, 20, 26) and tells them, "Do not be afraid" (Mt 28:10). He chides them for their disbelief, urges them to believe "that it is I myself" (Lk 24:39), and exhorts Thomas, "Do not be unbelieving, but believe" (Jn 20:27). Strengthened by the grace of the risen Lord, Saint Peter can encourage his people during a time of persecution, "Cast all your worries upon him because he cares for you... Resist [the Devil], steadfast in faith, knowing that your fellow believers throughout the world undergo the same sufferings. The God of all grace... will himself restore, confirm, strengthen, and establish you after you have suffered little" (1 Pt 5:7-10[11]).

❧

How, then, can we better practice mutual encouragement in Christ amid our various doubts, fears, and discouraging trials? First, we need to acknowledge that God is the source of all encouragement; without His grace we can neither receive nor extend encouragement. By and large, we are not called to solve others' problems; much of the time we cannot even solve our own! However, we can, like Saint Paul (2 Cor 1:4), pass on to others the encouragement that we have received from God. We can make time and space for others, listen to others' groans, and take them to heart. We can refrain from whining about our own trials or the crosses that others seem to lay upon us. It may be appropriate, however, to share how wondrously God has led us through our afflictions. If we have the authority and the

---

11   Used on the Feast of Saint Mark

opportunity, we might be able to invite people who feel left out to attend certain community gatherings. We might be able to point out faults gently and prudently, or discerningly to ask others to correct and encourage. We might be able to solicit the opinions of those who feel powerless. Perhaps most of all, we can strive to pursue zealous prayer lives, both in private and in public, so that we set a good example that may help to enkindle renewed enthusiasm in others for living in radiant faith. Christian encouragement is not a matter of making people feel good, patching over problems, or eliminating difficulties, but of leading people humbly and gracefully to the God who deeply shares our every concern. At the same time, we as Oblates and monks need to remember that our Oblation or monastic profession, far from being a "feather in our caps," is a grace-filled commitment to welcome Christ to stretch us and encourage us in every way He chooses to become the living sacrifices of praise that He wants us to be. In the process of encouraging others according to the plan of God, we ourselves receive encouragement and strength to resist complacency. As we put aside the impatience and anger that tend to discourage others, we can strengthen our mutual desire to know Jesus Christ and His immense love for us all. As Saint John did in his Gospel, our words and example can move others to "believe that Jesus is the Messiah, the Son of God, so that through this belief [we] may have life in his name" (Jn 20:31).

∽

P.S.: When I was writing this essay, I received a phone call from a distressed single mother who lives far away. She shared with me her immeasurably heavy burdens and the several difficult decisions she faces. From my perspective as a monk who has almost no experience in such matters, I could offer her no practical answers; but I hope and pray that my listening and our praying together over the phone may have given this good Christian woman some encouragement to keep trusting the God who sustains her.

11

---⬡⬡⬡---

THE CHALLENGE TO REVERENCE
GOD, PEOPLE, AND SACRED PLACES

I T is sometimes said that we live in an age characterized by a loss
of reverence. Many people seem to be deprived of a sense of the
sacred and even of common courtesies, which are a springboard
into the holy. Likewise, what was once considered poor in taste or
even blasphemous has become commonplace and acceptable to
many. Language that was once deemed offensive or sinful has become
standard in the media. Formalities that were considered normal at
meals or in public places are now generally ignored. Even in churches
it can be difficult to find reverence and a sense of awe; casual speech,
casual dress, and casual behavior have taken the place of silence (or
occasional hushed words), Sunday-best clothes, and carefully ex-
ecuted gestures and attentive postures. How can we begin to address
this situation?

❧

One day after our daily monastic Mass in the Archabbey Basilica,
I became irritated over some unusually loud conversations that were
taking place. While some worshipers were trying to pray after Mass,
others were chatting at length, perhaps about very legitimate matters but with a very audible volume. As it happened, later that day I
needed to deliver some liturgical booklets to the seminary chapel to
prepare for our monastic Evening Prayer. When I went to the chapel
with a box of booklets right after breakfast, I found a number of

seminarians praying quietly before their Mass. It probably occurred to me that I could have deposited the booklets in the chapel later in the day; yet I was anxious to get them out of my hands then and there. In putting the box on a shelf and adjusting a few other things in that location, I made some commotion, and then I realized that I could be disrupting the seminarians' prayer. I saw how my desire for convenience and comfort could lead me to abuse others' need for reverence and sacred silence. Critical though I could be of others' lack of reverence, I myself could be guilty of causing unnecessary commotion in an oratory.

℘

Saint Benedict gives high priority to reverence in the monastery and especially in the oratory, the place of common prayer, and so he legislates for it. He stipulates, "The oratory ought to be what it is called [a place of prayer], and nothing else is to be done or stored there."[1] Furthermore, "after the Work of God, all should leave in complete silence and with reverence for God, so that a brother who may wish to pray alone will not be disturbed by the insensitivity of another."[2] Here we see a two-fold reason for maintaining a quiet atmosphere in the oratory: reverence for God Himself and charitable consideration for those who wish to pray without disturbance. In a rare reference to gestures, Saint Benedict mentions in Chapter 9 on the Night Office, "let all the monks rise from their seats in honor and reverence for the Holy Trinity."[3] The monks are likewise to "stand with respect and awe"[4] when the Gospel is read at Vigils. Saint Benedict reminds his monks that praying the Liturgy of the Hours is a holy activity; although "we believe that the divine presence is everywhere,"[5] "we should believe this to be especially true when we celebrate the divine office."[6] Therefore, the monks will hasten to

---

1   RB 52:1
2   RB 52:2-3
3   RB 9:7
4   RB 11:9
5   RB 19:1
6   RB 19:2

attend the Office "with all dignity and decorum."[7] In Chapter 20, on "Reverence in Prayer," Saint Benedict insists that we "lay our petitions before the Lord God of all things with the utmost humility and sincere devotion."[8] It is the interior attitude that matters most; "we must know that God regards our purity of heart and tears of compunction, not our many words."[9]

Of course, reverence in the oratory does not exclude the need for reverence in other places and in other situations as well. The whole atmosphere of a monastery should be one of reverence for God, who is ever-present; reverence for other people; and reverence even for material things. Monks are to recognize the power of God working whenever they perceive the achievement of something good; "it is the Lord's power, not their own, that brings about the good in them."[10] They are to treat their abbot with respect because "he is believed to hold the place of Christ in the monastery."[11] The title *abbot* comes from the Latin word *abba*, which Christ used to address God the Father and which the early monks also applied to Christ. The abbot himself must stand in awe of his sacred responsibility; he "must always remember what he is and remember what he is called."[12] The younger monks are also to be respected and heard at community meetings because "the Lord often reveals what is better to the younger."[13] Monks believe that God speaks to them through their superiors,[14] and "any requests to a superior should be made with all humility and respectful submission."[15] The brothers are urged to have appropriate reverence for the "utensils and goods of the monastery," to treat them "as sacred vessels of the altar,"[16] to keep them clean, and to handle them carefully.[17] If material things are to be treated

7	RB 22:6
8	RB 20:2
9	RB 20:3
10	RB Prologue:29
11	RB 2:2
12	RB 2:30
13	RB 3:3
14	RB 5:4-6, 5:9, 5:15, 7:34
15	RB 6:7
16	RB 31:10
17	RB 32:4

with intentional care, how much more should people be honored and reverenced, especially because Christ is present in them! The cellarer "must show every care and concern for the sick, children, guests, and the poor."[18] The sick should be "truly served as Christ"[19] and "out of honor for God."[20] Guests, too, are to be received with gratitude and awe; all of them "are to be welcomed as Christ,"[21] and community members are most especially to show "great care and concern... in receiving poor people and pilgrims, because in them more particularly Christ is received."[22] Every monk is to live with "the fear of God always before his eyes,"[23] and Saint Benedict demands this quality in particular from the deans,[24] the cellarer,[25] the infirmarian,[26] and the guest master.[27] Thus monks are to live in sacred awe of the presence of God in all circumstances, and this reverential awe is to be reflected in their demeanor in sacred spaces, in their handling of things, and in their interactions with other people, especially superiors and needy people.

೧೨

How are we, then, to grow in reverence for what is sacred? How are we to maintain a holy awe for sacred spaces and to allow this reverence to overflow into our dealings with people and our utilizing of material things? Most of us have little or no authority for imposing silence in a church or for ensuring that the environment in a worship space be awe-inspiring. Each of us, however, can provide a good example for others and play his or her small part, with charity, to counteract the sense of unholy casualness that has invaded so many of our churches.

---

18   RB 31:9
19   RB 36:1
20   RB 36:4
21   RB 53:1
22   RB 53:15
23   RB 7:10
24   RB 21:1-2
25   RB 31:2
26   RB 36:7
27   RB 53:21

Here at Saint Vincent we have almost no rules for maintaining silence or other manifestations of reverence in our basilica or chapels; so I certainly am not about to make suggestions for rules for others. However, from what I have seen and read, I gather that certain attitudes and practices can help to nurture reverence in our sacred spaces and elsewhere. For example, before and after Mass or other church services, we can strive to maintain silence, both interior and exterior. Coming early or staying late can give us opportunities to prepare prayerfully for the service or, after the service, to allow its graces to overflow into daily life. During prayer we can strive to maintain inner silence and reverent attention by keeping our bodies in positions that help us to be alert and receptive to God's word. For example, we can avoid slouching or stretching our limbs into awkward positions. We can make our bows, genuflections, and other gestures deliberate and thought-filled so that our hearts are stirred to deeper worship and our whole beings are really honoring God through liturgical actions. We can sing with genuine joy and yet with a becoming restraint that keeps us from *sticking out like a sore thumb*, especially if our voice tends to be loud or out of tune. In both recitation and song we can try our best to be in synchronization with others as a reminder that we are growing in communion with our fellow worshipers and also helping to render the liturgy graceful, beautiful, and symbolic of the heavenly liturgy into which our earthly liturgy aims to enter. Reverence in our hearts and minds and reverent actions with our bodies can assist us in making genuine contact with God and in having "our minds... in harmony with our voices"[28] when we pray.

Are there times when we ought to talk in sacred spaces? Of course, there are emergencies. Furthermore, we sometimes see people at worship whom we do not encounter elsewhere, and there may be a need to communicate something to them softly. In such a case we should try, if possible, to bring the conversation outside or into a hallway beyond the formal worship space. If we really must talk in the church itself, our conversation should be brief and to the point, and without ongoing chat about incidental matters. Although whispering is

---

28   RB 19:7

better than loud talk, even whispers during a service with readings and silent pauses can be very disruptive, especially in places like our basilica, where sounds carry very easily. A prolonged conversation of whispers at one end of a building can readily upset people who are trying to pray at the other end of the building. Although occasional talk may seem necessary, the general rule should be to maintain "esteem for silence"[29] and to speak only "seriously and with becoming modesty, briefly and reasonably."[30]

At the same time we must learn to be patient with those who disturb us through conversation or other forms of apparent irreverence. Certainly, outside of the time for worship there are necessary disturbances in churches. Maintenance people must operate sweepers and floor-polishers. Masters of ceremonies, organists, and cantors must sometimes practice. Tour-leaders must usher groups through and give explanations. Construction workers must proceed on renovations, sometimes even during services. The noises from these functions must be accepted cheerfully and, if possible, even incorporated into our prayer. The one praying may be able to grow in the realization that prayer amid undesirable commotion can be just as valid as prayer amid awesome silence. Does not God look more into the heart than at a restless body or at uncontrollably ruffled emotions? One can also remember that nothing can "separate us from the love of God that comes to us in Christ" (Rom 8:39), including noisy machinery or boisterous people. We can pray for people who offend our sense of reverence, and we can strive to maintain peace in our hearts no matter what happens. How inappropriate it would be to intend to honor God, who is love, by nurturing judgmental, unloving thoughts before, during, or after a worship service in His house! Yes, in His good zeal, Our Lord drove out merchants and overturned tables in the Jewish temple because His Father's "house of prayer" had been turned into a "den of thieves" (Mk 11:17[†]). We, however, who are not so pure in intention, are unlikely to be called to such prophetic action. As sinners, it is we who first must cleanse the temples of our bodies, and of our hearts and minds, and then take action to enhance

29   RB 6:2
30   RB 7:60

reverence in a given situation with patience and charity in the ways in which God may lead us. Most of us do not have authority to make regulations for worship spaces, and it is probably just as well.

℘

In the end, learning to have reverence and to show reverence is a matter of love. Our desire to maintain a sacred atmosphere in sacred places—and in dealings with people and things—needs to be a response of love to the all-holy God who loved us first. Indeed, may our every worship space become what it is called, a place of prayer; but may *we* also become what we are called—"a holy nation, a people [God] claims for his own…" (1 Pt 2:9[†]) and "living stones, built as an edifice of spirit, into a holy priesthood, offering spiritual sacrifices acceptable to God through Jesus Christ" (1 Pt 2:5[†]). Those of us who are Oblates are committed in a special way to make our whole lives an offering of love, praise, and thanksgiving to God. We become authentic oblations to God and authentic Christians when we are filled with new life in Christ, when we seek holiness, when we treat sacred things as sacred, and when we show reverence for all people and all creation. In counteracting the prideful irreverence of our age, we also need to offer ourselves in a zealous nurturing of humility with our whole beings. We thus make it clear to ourselves and to others—with joy and gratitude—that God is God and we are not God. We are called to nurture this reverence, in the way appropriate to each situation, whether we are "at the Work of God, in the oratory, the monastery or the garden, or on a journey or in the field, or anywhere else."[31] When we deliberately make of ourselves a living sacrifice of praise in all circumstances, we become the reverent, loving creatures that we were meant to be and help others to do the same.

℘

A beautiful article "The Eucharist and Silence" from a lecture given by Father Laurence Freeman, O.S.B.,[32] reminds us that reverence and

---

31   RB 7:63
32   Lecture at The School of Prayer, Archdiocese of Melbourne. April 20, 2005.

silence in liturgy have a profound effect on the way Christians bring justice and peace to the world.

> *Silence is not merely the absence of noise but the spirit of loving attention... Silence as a liturgical experience... draws the community closer together and unifies their attention so that together in mind and heart they can hear the word and share in the mystery... Silence in the Eucharist, understood spiritually not legalistically, exposes the power of the sacrament as an empowerment of justice and peace... Pope John Paul's vision of liturgical silence expanded into his insight into contemporary spirituality. 'The spread, also outside Christian worship, of practices of meditation that give priority to recollection is not accidental. Why not start with pedagogical daring a specific education in silence within the coordinates of personal Christian experience?' (Spiritus et Sponsa).*[33]

෮

Let us more and more educate ourselves in reverence and silence so that we may dwell ever more fully in the mystery of God's love in the celebration of the Eucharist, in the halls of every worship space, and ultimately at all times and in all places.

---

33   *Spiritus et Sponsa*, Pope John Paul II. December 4, 2003.

12

CASTING OUT FEAR

AMONG the dangers of the spiritual life are two apparent opposites: the attitude that we have been perfected beyond improvement and, in contrast, the fear that we are so hopelessly deficient that God cannot help us to progress further. The first condition is one of pride, and so is the second although it masks itself as humility. Our task as Christians is to trust totally in God's merciful love despite our abysmal weakness and sinfulness and to hope that, in cooperation with God's graces, He will lead us to the heights of perfection. Moreover, God does want us ultimately to be perfect in the way of Christ. Our Lord calls us to be "perfect as your heavenly Father is perfect" (Mt 5:48[†]) and to "love the Lord your God with all your heart, with all your soul, with all your mind, and with all your strength" (Mk 12:30[†]). Of course, this *perfection* is in terms of love, mercy, and compassion. We are surely never to become all-powerful and all-knowing as God is. We shall always be creatures, and He our Creator and Redeemer; and that is part of our joy! The mystery of Christ's Resurrection assures us of the victory of Christ's self-emptying love and the victory of His gift of hope in us, the hope of sharing as fully as we can in the Blessed Trinity's communion of love.

Saint Benedict wisely challenges us to aspire to the summit of perfect love. After laying out the twelve steps of humility, he asserts that the monk who ascends all these steps "will quickly arrive at that perfect love of God which casts out fear."[1] Here he is quoting from 1 Jn 4:18[†], which in full reads, "Love has no room for fear; rather, perfect love casts out all fear. And since fear has to do with punishment, love is not yet perfect in one who is afraid." In these passages Saint John and Saint Benedict are not speaking of the genuine "fear of the Lord," a humble reverence and awe that acknowledges that God is God and we are not; this fear is a salutary and necessary part of the spiritual journey. Rather, they are referring to the fear that arises from focus on ourselves and preoccupation with our limitations, weakness, and unworthiness, all of which stem from a lack of trust in God's generous bounty. This fear makes it difficult to love. When we fear what others think about us, how few resources we have, or how likely we are to fail, we exclude the possibilities opened by God's lavish love, and we thus block off some channels of His grace.

☙

Last fall I was often preoccupied with the project of ordering copies of a book, and it made me aware of the negative impact of fears in me, fears that still need to be conquered. After I put a notice in the Oblate newsletter, some 60 books were ordered, and then more people requested books at our local Oblate meeting in September; so I ordered 80 books. Well, October came, November came, and December came; and still no books had arrived. Whenever I contacted the company, I would receive a polite reply: "The books *will* come; it's just taking us some time to get them. Our company is undergoing reorganization." At one point, however, a notice came to me in the mail saying that the book was out of stock. Well, that notice really stirred up my fears and anger! What did I fear? I feared coping with the embarrassment that would come from failure in a project that I had initiated. I feared losing the trust of people who had depended on me for obtaining the books. I feared being immersed in a tendency to blame myself with very little mercy. And I feared all the extra work involved in refunding hundreds of dollars to disappointed individuals. (For me, having to undo something I have done with

---

1   RB 7:67

considerable investment of time and energy is dreadful!) As it turned out, the company soon thereafter informed me that the notice had been in error; and then, shortly before Christmas, I was notified that 100 copies of the book had arrived from England, that they would be shipped to the Oblate Office promptly, and that we would be given an even greater discount than had been offered earlier, with a cost of $10.36 per book instead of $18.00 per book. The books came in late December and early January. I rejoiced! I had refund checks made out to all the purchasers and gathered two Oblate volunteers, who generously offered several hours of their time to package the books for mailing or for personal distribution. As new fears cropped up within me, I then realized that freedom from fear must not depend on a positive outcome, but rather must arise from a choice to trust and to receive with humility whatever God gives. I had a new choice, either to lament all the extra work and extra communication and the loss of *my time* that came with the distribution of books and checks, or to welcome the signs of God's love in the company's apologies, in their offer of a generous discount, in their friendly disposition on the phone, and in the volunteers' magnanimous offer of assistance. (Furthermore, when I say "company," I must realize that this means real human beings created in God's image!)

ॐ

What, then, is the remedy for our fears? It is growth in trust in God's superabundant love, in a humble acceptance of our own radical poverty, and in a humble risk-taking that acts on the belief that when we make decisions in good faith, God will *come through* in His way and His time, which is always better than our way and our time. Especially in the twelve steps of humility, the *Holy Rule* provides insightful guidance for living in a love that grows gradually and that becomes strong enough to cast out fears one by one. If we embrace the fear of the Lord recommended by the first step of humility, we come to remember how lovingly He guides us each moment of every day and thus also how He works against our fears and anxieties related to loss of control. If we learn the second step's exhortation to surrender our will more and more to the Lord's will, we overcome the fear of not getting our way and learn that His way is always far better for us. Likewise, in the third step, when obedience to a superior for love of Christ demands that we die to self in a painful way (or even die physically for the One who loved us first), we see how Christ's love can cast out our fear of death and loss of self-will. So, too, God's love overcomes our fear of adversities and injustices (step 4), our fear of letting others know our sins and weaknesses (step 5), our fear of losing others' esteem (steps 6 and 7), our fear of losing our uniqueness among others (step 8), our fear of being less valued because we lack cleverness in speech and readiness to laugh (steps 9, 10, and 11), and our fear of exposing our sins to God's awesome but merciful judgment (step 12). When we learn more and more how unshakable is God's love for us, our fears may still emerge from time to time, but they no longer have much control over us. Christ's love begins to reign supreme in us, and our humble submission to the power of His love will be fulfilled in the new life of resurrection for which we yearn.[2]

I found this principle of love's power to cast out fear to be manifest in a concrete way in my experience of attending the papal Mass in Washington, DC. One by one my fears were addressed by the loving intervention of God in ways that I could not have predicted. In the first place I did not even want to go because I feared the loss of time needed for my work, but then God seemed to nudge me to sign my name on the list of pilgrim monks. Then, before the day of the trip and even during the trip, I worried about the burden of long-range travel, the uncertainty of overnight accommodations, the danger of food that might upset my system, the possible confusion in using public transportation amid crowds of people, the lack of customary facilities on the field of a large baseball stadium, the difficulty of bearing with bright sunlight in an open field, and the need to find the monks, amid a large crowd, with whom I was to travel home. In every situation the love of God worked through people and situations to render my fears useless. In the end, it did not even matter that at one point I lost my ticket and then left behind a coat in the vesting room.

2   RB 7

Such things, I realized, are of miniscule importance when compared to the opportunity to surrender our whole beings to God's all-magnanimous love, especially in a Holy Eucharist celebrated under the leadership of Pope Benedict himself and in communion with a huge, enthusiastic congregation representing the whole Church. Indeed, God's love was truly manifest in the Holy Father, in the Mass itself, in the warmth of the people around me, and in the innumerable incidents that led me to enter a bit better into the communion of love that casts out fear. Now I must continue to trust that the love that led me safely to a marvelous experience at Nationals Park and back to the Archabbey will continue to embrace me and infuse my every experience so as to teach me the uselessness of every fear that tends to enslave me.

℘

What, then, is our role in welcoming the "perfect love of God"[3] to overcome our particular fears? It is our daily struggle to live in faith, hope, and love and in the humility that summons us to rely continually on God's grace. First, of course, we need to admit that we do sometimes live in fear. It might be helpful to learn our particular fears and to work on them one by one. When we recognize a fear coming to the surface, we can invite Christ our risen Lord to rule over that fear in His victorious love. We may not feel or understand His saving work in us, but repeated surrender of our fears to Him will give Him a chance to enter ever more deeply into those areas of our lives where we cling to self-sufficient ways and lack trust. Another help might be to remember, in prayer, those past circumstances when God in His great love rescued us from our distress and made it clear how futile it was to fear and to waste time in worry. Then we need to trust, trust, and trust again that the same love that lifted us up in the past is still ever-present, all-powerful, and ever eager to reveal itself to us. When the love of Christ begins to fill our hearts, it leaves less and less room for fear, regardless of how dismal our external circumstances may be. Then we can hope that someday we shall reach a point at which

---

3   RB 7:67

we do everything "out of love for Christ, good habit, and delight in virtue."[4]

༽

The beautiful Gospel readings for Masses during this Easter Season assure us that Christ is indeed risen and is inviting us to partake of the greatest joy we can imagine: a share in His own eternal communion of love with the Father in the Holy Spirit. The Lord Jesus wants to take us with Him to the Father, "that where I am you also may be" (Jn 14:3[†]). This place with the Father is not only held out as a promise for the future, although our state of heavenly "rest" with God will certainly exceed anything we can experience here on earth. This state of loving communion begins here and now as we come to believe that Christ is in the Father and in us; as we allow ourselves to be guided by the Spirit of truth; as we share in the very works that Christ does in and through us (Jn 14:12[†]); and as we trust ever more fully that God never leaves us orphaned (Jn 14:18[†]). Let us, then, rejoice daily in the ways in which God summons us to a deeper humility. Let us, in that humility, aspire to the perfect love that casts out fear and to the joy that flows from that love. Rather than murmur over inconveniences and tragedies, let us welcome the Lord to overcome our fear and lack of trust and to dwell in us as He keeps expanding our hearts in the love that knows no bounds and that becomes our joy and our delight.

13

SAINT BENEDICT AND THE CROSS: PUTTING ASIDE OUR OWN CONCERNS AND LEAVING THINGS UNFINISHED

s I began to compose this essay about Saint Benedict and the Cross, I looked over the pamphlet that we give to newly invested Oblate novices along with a medal of Saint Benedict. To my surprise and dismay, I noticed that the pamphlet's pages were in the wrong order. It took me a while to discover that the text on the front continues not on the next page but on another page. My first impulse was to plan to reassemble the master copy right away to eliminate all confusion. (When I discover any errors, I tend to want to set everything right in an instant!) On the other hand, common sense and prudence dictated that I allow the error to remain for the time being because I had plenty of other projects of higher priority. I must simply trust that Oblates and Oblate novices who have the pamphlet will have the ingenuity to read the pages in the proper order, and, even more importantly, I must trust that God will lead me to make the corrections in His time and His way. I had to let go of my impulse to straighten out everything now. Again and again, I must embrace the cross of leaving something unfinished.

The process of revising our monastic Divine Office, which has been going on for over two years, presents a similar situation. (How I wish it were all done right now!) Despite all efforts to proofread drafts of each master booklet, errors have appeared after the printing of the booklets in every instance. (In several cases the company that prints the booklets mysteriously received a file with uncorrected psalm texts and music; so we ended up having six hundred booklets with a huge number of errors.) Under such circumstances it is tempting to go to one of two extremes: (1) to throw up one's hands in despair and give up on the whole effort or (2) to begin hasty, frantic efforts to correct all the errors as soon as is humanly possible. In either case, I would be plunging myself into slavery to my concerns and my will instead of calming down, reexamining my frenzied emotions, and truly seeking God and His will in the whole matter, as weighed against other responsibilities that He has given me.

༄

The word "cross" (*crux* in Latin) does not appear even once in the *Holy Rule*; and yet the text of the *Rule* has a number of references to the Passion of Christ, which make it clear that the life of a Benedictine must be a continual taking up of one's crosses in communion with Christ. The Prologue reminds us that in faithfully observing Christ's teachings, "we shall through patience share in the sufferings of Christ."[1] In the "Instruments of Good Works," the monk is told: "Renounce yourself in order to follow Christ."[2] That is, the monk is to embrace the cross of self-denial in order to go wherever Christ leads him. In Chapter 5 on obedience, Saint Benedict cites Mt 7:14 and reminds the monk, "Narrow is the road that leads to life."[3] Of course, that is the road of the Cross. The one explicit reference to Our Lord's death occurs in Chapter 7, where Saint Benedict describes ideal obedience to a superior as being done "for the love of God" and in imitation of "the Lord of whom the Apostle says: 'He became obedient even to death.'"[4] Also, Saint Benedict's many exhortations about being patient[5] can be taken to imply a sharing in Christ's own

---

1   RB Prologue:50
2   RB 4:10
3   RB 5:11
4   Phil 2:8, RB 7:34
5   *e.g.* RB 2:25, 7:35, 36:5, 58:3, 68:2, 72:5

patience, which culminated in His bearing all of humanity's sufferings on the Cross.

The medal of Saint Benedict, which displays an image of a cross, engages us in the struggle against evil through the inscriptions on the medal. The Latin initials on the arms of the cross, CSSML, mean in English, "May the holy Cross be my light! May the dragon [Satan] never be my guide!" The margin around the cross has the initials VRSNSMV and SMQLIVB, which can be translated, "Begone, Satan! Tempt me not with your vanities! What you offer me is evil. Drink the poisoned cup yourself!" Both sayings assert that our Christian struggle against evil is real, that evil must be resisted firmly and persistently, and that the Cross is our weapon against evil. Therefore, when each day we encounter sufferings of various sorts and are tempted to become angry, to complain or blame, or to give in to depression, the spirituality of the Cross urges us to *offer up* the sufferings in union with Christ on the Cross. He shares our pain and distress and gives us every grace to let go of futile human strivings and to entrust the whole situation to God the Father in union with Him. We need to calm our anxieties and fears. We need to call upon Christ relentlessly for the grace to ward off self-centered thoughts and feelings. We need to make acts of faith in God, with confidence that He is working to bring good out of our painful situation. Thus we already share in the fruits of the Resurrection even while we bear our crosses. Satan would drive us into discouragement or rebellious self-sufficiency. Our loving God in His mercy encourages us to keep walking in a faith that will lead to ultimate glory, of which we already have a tentative taste.

☙

How, then, are we to respond to the pieces of unfinished business that we have in our lives? Should we just give up on the projects, or should we feverishly attack them? First, it might be helpful to realize that even when we think we have finished a task, there still remains more to be done. Most of us like to have a sense of closure to our tasks, but, in truth, we cannot bring anything to perfection by our own efforts. Even the most beautiful and complete work on earth is poor, incomplete, and flawed in comparison with God's all-perfect activity. What we fail to bring to completion, however, God will complete in His way and His time, as long as we cooperate with Him. Perhaps God will choose someone else to carry on what we have begun. As Saint Paul said to the Philippians, "I am sure of this much: that he who has begun the good work in you will carry it through to completion, right up to the day of Christ Jesus" (Phil 1:6[†]). On the other hand, God certainly wants us, with joy and good zeal, to do our part in every worthy project. He expects us to cooperate with His graces and to try our best to do things in His way.

Secondly, when we find ourselves frustrated over unfulfilled goals, we need to focus more on the Lord Jesus and His Cross, a sign of His immense love, rather than on ourselves and our misery. The latter leads only to bitterness, hopelessness, and greater anxiety. The former directs us to a growing communion of love with Christ and a growing joy in the opportunity to share in His Cross. As Saint Paul boldly asserts, "For, to me, 'life' means Christ; hence dying is so much gain" (Phil 1:21[†]). Is not one form of "dying" the letting go of stubborn insistence that a project be completed in my way and according to my timetable? Furthermore, we can grow in wisdom to discern more carefully between our plans and God's will for us. We may very well think that we are proceeding according to His will, but then He may reveal to us that we need to drop our project temporarily or permanently. Perhaps, for His own good reasons, He wanted us to begin an endeavor and then to leave it. What we know that God really wants is our whole self—our will, our mind, our heart, and our total response to His ineffable love. He wants us, through the ordinary events of daily life, to be drawn into an ever deeper communion with Himself. That is indeed our glory! As we heard at Mass on the Second Sunday of Ordinary Time, "You shall be a glorious crown in the hand of the Lord, a royal diadem held by your God... As a young man marries a virgin, your Builder shall marry you; and as a bridegroom rejoices in his bride, so shall your God rejoice in you" (Is 62: 3, 5[†]).

Those of us who are Oblates, Oblate novices, or monks presumably entered into our vocation because we wanted to give ourselves totally to God, to become people of deep prayer, and to grow in generous love for others in the pattern of Christ's own sacrificial love.

Our valid desire to please God in everything, which perhaps was very intense at the outset, may have been sparked by an emotionally rewarding experience; this may have led us to think that we were already willing and able to do God's will in everything. Most likely, we subsequently realized how imperfect our motives were and how many other, less worthy desires we still had. We wanted to please God, but often we had (and still have) our own ideas about how and when to fulfill what we think to be His will. The coming of crosses can help to detach us from self-centered thoughts, feelings, and desires; they can help to reduce the "me" in whatever we plan and do. Little by little we can learn to let go quickly of whatever we want to do and to embrace joyfully whatever new direction God has in store for us. We can let Him rule more and more over our impulses that can so easily lead us away from loving communion with Him.

Thirdly, the Cross, the Gospel, and the *Rule* arm us powerfully to deal with our chronic faults. It may be that we would like to rid ourselves instantly of a tendency to talk too much, of a recurring preoccupation with our health, of temptations to overindulge in food, of a lamentable habit of arriving late, of a long-standing resistance to finding enough time to pray, of a desire to dominate conversations, or of any of many other seemingly insuperable flaws. Our desire to overcome these quickly is commendable. However, if we are doing our best to struggle against sinful tendencies and to trust in God's ever-available help and forgiveness, then it may be even better to accept, with humility and peace, our very slow progress in improving. Why does God not take these away instantly? His ways are mysteriously different from ours. The Scriptures and the Church's long spiritual traditions hint that God may be challenging us to grow in humility. Perhaps He is showing us how to trust more in Him and less in ourselves. Perhaps He is teaching us to long more for eternity, when we shall be truly free. (Along with Saint Teresa of Avila, it might be valuable for us to see life on this earth as "one overnight stay in a bad inn.") Perhaps God is using our flaws to help us not to judge others whom we might consider less virtuous than ourselves. In any case, God is certainly urging us to unite the sufferings linked to our chronic faults with the sufferings of Christ on the Cross. In doing so, we are to leave behind murmuring, worry about what other people think, worry about how and when God will intervene, and preoccupation with how well we are coping. With the graces flowing from the Cross, we can learn to accept the loving embrace of our crucified Lord to heal us and purify us in His way and His time. Just as Saint Benedict's monks were to "put aside their work to be ready for the second signal [for prayer],"[6] so are we to put aside our worries and fears concerning our miserably imperfect spiritual condition, as long as we are doing our best to cooperate with God's lavish outpouring of graces.

co

In his Christmas letter to Oblates affiliated with Saint John's Abbey, Oblate director Father Michael Kwatera, O.S.B., addressed the issue of "wanting it all" at Christmas time. In contrast to people's desire to grasp possessions, power, and popularity, Father Michael noted:

> [the birth of Jesus] *is the clearest proof that God wants to give us all that God has to give: God's very self given to us in Jesus the Lord. The Savior born for us is more than we could ever want, ever deserve, ever ask for. God's gift of God's Son at Christmas was not what the chosen people were expecting—not a political liberator but a Suffering Servant of God who would save humanity from sin and death.*

It was in giving up His very life on the Cross that Our Lord gained "all" for us. So, we need not fret that we do not yet have the "all" of spiritual perfection as seen from our very limited perspective.

co

When Lent approaches, it is especially appropriate to look to the Cross and to learn from Saint Benedict's devotion to it. The ashes we may receive are a healthful reminder that although we shall die

---

6   RB 48:12

and return to dust, if we join ourselves to Christ in traveling through this vale of tears, our share in His Cross brings us into a wonderful communion with Him even now. In Christ and with Christ we can ready ourselves to put aside our own concerns, to embrace the cross of obedience, and to gain the everlasting inheritance He has prepared for us. It is with Christ that we suffer. It is with Christ that we prepare for a holy death. It is with Christ that we are ready to die and be purified in Purgatory with total surrender to His ways. It is with Christ that we struggle daily with our crosses and avoid the twin dangers of overconfidence and despair. It is with Christ that even now, amid all our miseries, we live in joyful hope of "hastening on to the perfection of monastic life"[7] and of some day arriving "at that perfect love of God which casts out fear."[8]

7   RB 73:2
8   RB 7:67

14

Aspiring to "Loftier Summits": Pursuing the Goal in Little Steps and Avoiding a Slide into Mediocrity

My current wristwatch, like some of my previous watches, tends to lose time gradually, perhaps a fraction of a second each day. I measure its accuracy by our church bells, because when I am at the organ I must finish playing the prelude before the 5:00 p.m. bell for Vespers. I can easily grow accustomed to the watch's being slow. One day the bell will ring at 4:59:55, then a few days later at 4:59:50, and some days later at 4:59:30. Of course, I could move the hands up a minute at any time, but I become so used to the inaccurately slow time that a part of me prefers it. Besides, if I set the watch forward, I might forget that I have done something new. Making such a change could be risky!

So can it be with our spiritual life. It can run down so gradually and imperceptibly that we can become comfortable with a mediocre regime of prayer and a less-than-intense relationship with God. At any stage in the slide into mediocrity, we could resolve to do something about it, but it can be easier to muse, "Perhaps tomorrow something will motivate me to go back to a more energetic practice of prayer." We forget that God is calling out to us daily—if not moment by moment. "If you hear his voice today, do not harden your hearts."[1]

---

1   Ps 95:8; RB Prologue:10

എ

A recent week was quite hectic for us monks here at Saint Vincent. We celebrated the investiture of four novices, the first profession of one monk, and the solemn profession of two monks. Many Oblates, their guests, and many other guests celebrated with us. After these ceremonies, our monastic community gathered for an intensive annual meeting. Then one of our monks was ordained a priest, and two were ordained deacons. Finally, a newly ordained priest offered a Mass of thanksgiving in the basilica. That was also the day of our monthly Oblate meeting for the Saint Gregory the Great Deanery.

After those six days of almost relentless activity and less private prayer than I would have liked, I was tempted to plunge into my backlog of work with violent ferocity so that I might put everything back in order—my order—quickly. Fortunately, Father Fred's homily at the Mass of thanksgiving for the newly ordained priest powerfully reminded me that the love of Jesus Christ must come before everything else. In every Christian vocation our love for one another and our mutual service become dry, empty, and self-centered unless such deeds are rooted in the love of Christ. Rooting ourselves in Christ means, of course, that we need to spend ample time in prayer and to strive for continual recollection. Our spiritual life must have top priority; and if an emergency calls us away from our normal regimen of prayer for one day or several days, we must return promptly to *keeping our little rule*.[2] Otherwise, we can almost imperceptibly lose our initial fervor, slip into mediocrity, and become enslaved to a dull, somewhat hopeless existence that is basically less than Christian.

The *Rule* of Saint Benedict boldly stirs us out of such complacency. The urgency of remaining focused on God pervades the *Rule*. Again and again the monk needs to admit that he has fallen away from God, but "the labor of obedience will bring you back to him."[3] In fact, "with his good gifts which are in us, we must obey him at all times."[4] Saint Benedict's frequent use of the word "run" highlights the importance of the goal of doing everything in communion with

---

2   RB 73:8
3   RB Prologue:2
4   RB Prologue:6

Christ and for God's glory: "we must run and do now what will profit us forever"; "we shall run on the path of God's commandments."[5] The abbot himself is challenged always to "seek first the kingdom of God and his justice."[6] "It is love" that must impel everyone "to pursue everlasting life,"[7] primarily through the narrow path of cheerful, unhesitating obedience in all things. A monk must "constantly remember everything God has commanded"[8] and should seek to "arrive at that perfect love of God that casts out fear."[9] Saint Benedict grants that we are only beginners, and as such we tend to "blush for shame at being so slothful, so unobservant, so negligent"[10] when we look to the high standards of the Church fathers and monastic spiritual masters. Nonetheless, he exhorts the monk and the Oblate to "[hasten] on to the perfection of monastic [or Christian] life,"[11] to "[hasten] toward [our] heavenly home,"[12] and to "set out for the loftier summits"[13] after having mastered the rudiments of Christian spirituality. All are to seek "the very heights of perfection,"[14] and to do that one must put "the love of Christ... before all else,"[15] "cherish Christ above all,"[16] and "prefer nothing whatever to Christ."[17]

Yes, Saint Benedict is known as a *master of moderation*; as he says in various places and in various ways, "All things are to be done with moderation on account of the fainthearted."[18] Our holy father does not wish to set such impossibly high standards for us fragile earthen vessels that we become discouraged and give up on the spiritual life. However, he does not want the fainthearted to remain fainthearted, and moderation does not mean mediocrity in the spiritual life. Like

---

5	RB Prologue:44, 49
6	Mt 6:33; RB 2:35
7	RB 5:10
8	RB 7:11
9	RB 7:67
10	RB 73:7
11	RB 73:2
12	RB 73:8
13	RB 73:9
14	RB 73:2
15	RB 4:21
16	RB 5:2
17	RB 72:11
18	RB 48:9

Our Lord Himself, Saint Benedict challenges every monk and every person to aim for perfection and to aspire to the loftier summits of doctrine and virtue. In this essay, I am stressing the importance of aiming for loftier summits because we are so prone to set our standards too low, to backslide, and to settle for dull mediocrity.

At the same time, however, we must acknowledge that the heights are reached through the taking of small, undramatic steps in response to grace. One Easter, I received a letter from a cousin in Lithuania. Since my competence in the Lithuanian language is minimal, a part of me dreaded the arduous process of writing back, although I knew that to respond promptly was good for me and for my cousin and her family. Initially, to motivate myself I placed the letter on an empty space on the desk in my monastic cell. Well, the letter remained in that place for over two months without my feeling much motivation to tackle the project of responding. I finally realized that my mere looking at the letter was not leading me to the "loftier heights" of actually writing a reply. Therefore, I took the letter, along with two dictionaries and a grammar book, to my office and began to translate the letter, bit by bit, and to formulate a response. The process took over a week. I learned once again that to achieve a "great task" (like writing a letter in a foreign language) we need to aim high but also to take small steps each day to achieve our goal, however imperfectly; and we are not to give in to discouragement at the lamentable slowness of our progress or lack of proficiency. The same holds for progress in prayer.

ତ

How, then, are we to advance toward the "loftier heights" in the concrete choices in daily life? Wherever we are, whatever we are doing, no matter how much or how little we have progressed in the spiritual life, we must respond to the call of "forgetting what lies behind [and] straining forward to what lies ahead… the prize of God's upward calling, in Christ Jesus" (Phil 3:13-14). Yes, we must continually "strain forward" in response to grace, albeit usually in little steps. What are some little steps that we can take each day? Keep custody over your thoughts and words. Dash all disordered thoughts and feelings against Christ as quickly as possible. Strive especially to turn away from murmuring. Savor a small portion of the *Rule* at a certain time each day. Practice *lectio divina*, daily if possible, for at least 15 minutes. Pray as much of the Liturgy of the Hours as you can, daily if possible; invite other family members to pray with you. Plan to make at least one retreat or several days of recollection each year. Whenever you feel annoyed at someone or something, pray instantly and say inwardly, "Praise God!" or "Thank You, Lord, for this little cross!" Whenever you encounter a disagreeable person, pray before you speak. Look for opportunities to pause by the Blessed Sacrament for at least a few minutes. If you are Catholic, go to confession often; also examine your conscience daily. Avoid mindless entertainment. Do not watch television unless the program is definitely edifying and moral. Avoid unnecessary shopping trips. Be careful with your time on the Internet, and flee quickly from anything indecent on it. Listen to the Lord continually as to where He wishes you to extend His love. Whenever you find yourself failing to meet your standards or slipping into discouragement, remember quickly "never [to] lose hope in God's mercy."[19]

≈

Some pertinent pieces of wisdom from Father Thomas Dubay's *Prayer Primer: Igniting a Fire Within*[20] are as follows:

> *Even if you are now on the lowest rung of sanctity, but are faithful to the light and love given you there, God will raise you to the next rung, and then the next, and the next.* (p. 150)

> *Growth in divine intimacy is not automatic, not simply a matter of getting on in years with no significant changes in how we live day by day.* (p. 176)

---

19   RB 4:74
20   Ignatius Press. San Francisco: 2003.

*We need to keep our eyes wide open to avoid the gradual slide
into mediocrity... The question to ask is: What must I do to
remain determined? No one else can do it for me.* (p. 177)

ↀ

"Straining forward," as Saint Paul says we must do, does not mean,
of course, that we are to push ourselves forward in spiritual growth so
that we "strain ourselves." It means, rather, that we continually and
prayerfully listen for the ways in which God is summoning us to put
away the old self and to be clothed anew with Christ. It means that
we daily "open our eyes" as best as we can "to the deifying light" and
that "with thunderstruck ears" we hear the divine voice calling us.[21]
Rather than laboring in vain or trying to keep guard over our lives by
our own efforts,[22] we learn that God "pours gifts on His beloved while
they slumber" (Ps 127:2[23]). Yes, we must do our part with all the energy and good zeal that we can muster, but it must be always in God's
will and in response to His grace. By aspiring to the loftier summits
under God's guidance, we come to possess the peace which is Christ's
gift to us (Jn 14:27), the peace that includes acceptance of the piti-
fully unremarkable progress we make each day and joyful hope in
reaching toward what "God has prepared for those who love him" (1
Cor 2:9). Thus "under God's protection"[24] we shall attain these lofty
and incomparably beautiful heights!

21　　　RB Prologue: 9-10, from Father Demetrius Dumm's translation
22　　　cf. Ps 127:1
23　　　Grail Psalter. GIA Publications. Chicago: 1963.
24　　　RB 73:9

15

CONDUCTING OURSELVES WITH PATIENCE: DYING TO SELF-CENTERED DEMANDS

W HEN as a child I was on shopping trips with my parents, we occasionally saw a customer who, being unhappy with a purchase, would approach a cashier or an exchange counter appearing angry, demanding, and, in my eyes, rather foolish. My father, who worked for 15 years as a salesman in a department store, would tell our family about his encounters with such people; sometimes they could be won over by kindness, but sometimes nothing could quell their impatient and often unreasonable demands. In witnessing such scenes and hearing such stories, I could only hope that I would never be such an impatient, demanding customer.

ℰ℘

Not long ago I was working on a project that I regarded as urgent, and one morning I approached our college's computer lab to print out some text that was essential for me for the pasting together of a booklet. I arrived at the scheduled opening time, but, alas, as sometimes is the case, the lab was not yet open. After waiting impatiently for a while, I went to a near-by office where I knew someone with a key to the lab, although he was not formally responsible for opening it. He graciously left his desk to unlock the lab for me. (Yes, I thought, I had overcome *that* obstacle!) When I went into the lab, however, I discovered that I had not brought my computer disk with me; so I had to go back to my office to retrieve it and thus "waste"

99

more precious time that I, in my enthusiasm, thought I should be using to advance my project. Well, I did finally have the text printed; but as the day wore on (and that term "wore on" is a tell-tale, loaded word that shows that I was not very open to grace), I seemed to find abundant reasons to murmur about other things' not going right and about my various tasks' falling further behind. Yes, on such days I am tempted to think, "Why does the world put such stumbling blocks in my way? Why can't I do my work without such painful delays and interruptions? Why do other people have to be so irresponsible? Why do computers sometimes require new passwords and yet not tell us customers how to put them in?" The list could go on and on. When you and I allow ourselves to become anxious and driven, it seems that "those irresponsible people" and "those things that don't work right" spoil our plans, make us reformulate our timetable (which was probably too rigid already), and render us irritable and even more anxious. Wouldn't it be such a simple solution if the rest of the world were to adjust to *my* very reasonable demands?

The problem and the answer, of course, do not reside so much in those outward circumstances as *inside me*. I choose to become impatient and demanding. I choose to draw up an inflexible schedule. I choose to keep thinking about all those unfinished projects instead of focusing on what I am doing now and enjoying the grace of the moment, even if my emotions are a bit frenzied. I choose to cling to the ridiculous idea that everything must "go right" for me today and that otherwise I have a right to display dismay and frustration so that the world will know how much *I* am suffering. So, too, it is my task to discover how to escape from the trap of making such poor choices and letting unfavorable situations rule over my disposition. Most especially, I must ask myself, "Is Jesus Christ the focus of my life at such times?" Furthermore, I must persist in asking this question, because my wayward self can easily go astray, even after the most uplifting periods of prayer. As the Letter to the Hebrews told us at Mass on the morning when I was writing this, "Remember the days past when, after you had been enlightened, you endured a great contest of suffering... Do not throw away your confidence; it will have great recompense. You need endurance to do the will of God and receive what He has promised... We are not among those who draw back and perish, but among those who have faith and will possess life" (Heb 10:32, 35-36, 39). To draw back is to allow selfish inner demands to govern us; to have faith is to welcome Christ to be our Lord and the Holy Spirit to guide us at every moment of the day. Yes, Our Lord may be calling us to grow particularly close to Him in those situations that most tax our patience.

୧୨

The *Holy Rule* does indeed have much to teach us about overcoming impatience, and in this, as in all its wisdom, it is totally focused on Christ. First of all, we learn, in Saint Benedict's quote of Rom 2:4, that God Himself is patient with us: "As the apostle says, 'Do you not know that the patience of God is leading you to repent?'"[1] If we were truly to realize how lovingly God puts up with our sins and faults and how hard He tries to put us back on course, we would have far less trouble dealing with the flaws of our fellow humans that "make us" impatient. Perhaps the key to all practice of patience is to know that it is a grace-filled participation in the sufferings of Christ. The monastic journey demands that, "we shall through patience share in the sufferings of Christ that we may deserve also to share in His kingdom."[2] Learning to be patient amid sufferings of various sorts is, therefore, essential in our lifelong pilgrimage of "putting on Christ" and overcoming self-centered demands, which characterize our "old," unconverted selves. With this principle in mind, we could almost relish those annoying situations that test our patience; by grace, they become opportunities to welcome Our Lord to heal the old wounds that underlie temptations to become demanding and impatient. The rest of the *Rule* abounds in practical examples. The fourth step of humility reminds us that we can, with grace, "quietly [embrace] suffering" and thus practice obedience (ultimately to God) "under difficult, unfavorable, or even unjust conditions."[3] It is encouraging to know that when we are "patient amid hardships and

---

1   RB Prologue:37
2   RB Prologue:50
3   RB 7:35

unjust treatment," we "are fulfilling the Lord's command" to turn the other cheek, to offer one's cloak, and to go the extra mile.[4] The instruments of good works reinforce this attitude: "Do not injure anyone, but bear injuries patiently."[5] Novice monks are to be "tested in all patience,"[6] presumably, as our wise novice master told us, not by artificial obstacles but simply by exposure to the ordinary ups and downs of daily life. Patiently bearing with sick brothers and serving them as Christ "leads [us] to a greater reward,"[7] presumably "greater" than the effect of serving someone who offers us positive feedback. A monk who has been asked to do a seemingly impossible job must not storm angrily into his superior's office but rather "explain patiently… the reasons why he cannot perform the task."[8] Most especially, we monks and Oblates grow in the good zeal that hastens us onward "to God and everlasting life"[9] by "supporting with the greatest patience one another's weaknesses of body or behavior."[10] Yes, the moment-to-moment practice of patience is—since "love is patient" (1 Cor 13:4)—the way to everlasting life!

☙

The struggle to become patient may be especially difficult amid our society's addiction to speed, efficiency, and supposed "rights." Yes, there are many instances of people whose dignity has been denied and who may justifiably "demand their rights," and it may indeed be God's call for any of us to help others to obtain rights to freedom of speech, to gainful employment, to the exercise of religious beliefs, and to deliverance from all sorts of oppression. However, in our day and in our individualistic society, we tend to demand, at least interiorly, supposed "rights" to plan our day however we wish, to eat whatever entices the eye or the palate, to purchase whatever makes life more convenient, to use nature in whatever way will add to personal

---

4	RB 7:42
5	RB 4:30
6	RB 58:11
7	RB 36:5
8	RB 68:2
9	RB 72:2
10	RB 72:5

comforts, and to yield to our insatiable desires in innumerable other ways. How can the Gospel, the teachings of the Church, and the *Rule* of Saint Benedict help to free us from those forces that tend to "make us" impatient and demanding? Once again, nothing really makes us react in such a way; we choose to give in to bad influences, however powerful they may be.

For one thing, in our *lectio divina* and in the Divine Office, we may rejoice and give thanks in solidarity with so many of God's people who have suffered enormous trials and, with God's grace, have learned to grow through them. Furthermore, we learn from the New Testament and the *Rule* that sufferings borne patiently draw us into deeper union with Christ in an especially powerful way. What marvelous encouragement! Likewise, we find many references to God's patience with His people; and examining our own consciences and reflecting on our past lives and all our infidelities, we can be grateful that God has led us forward so mercifully and helped us to repent. Also, it is encouraging that even if we overcome impatience in one area of our lives, we shall probably struggle with impatience in some other realms for the rest of our earthly lives. That, too, is really good news since our strivings to become patient keep us on the narrow road to salvation and prevent us from becoming too self-confident. At the same time, we can learn amid this struggle that we don't have to give in to the demands of our unhealed old selves; by putting on Christ and dashing our negative impulses against Him, we can, in the power of His love, be victorious even amid the most unfavorable circumstances and amid our own unruly thoughts and feelings. We don't have to get upset in any given situation and "demand our rights." In fact, we can even be glad when others' weaknesses of body or behavior challenge our patience, for therein lie marvelous opportunities to dismiss our unloving impulses, to welcome Our Lord in His Passion to be at our side, and to begin, with His grace, to practice the same patient love that He displayed during His trial and on the way to Calvary and that He displays now to us.

As for impatience with our own inability to accomplish what we once thought we had to accomplish, which is one of my glaring weaknesses, we might repeatedly try to refocus on the one thing we are doing, as God's gift of the moment, and chase away worries about the past and the future. Practicing such recollection, which for us Christians is really a continual refocusing on Christ and His redeeming love at each moment, can help us to overcome the fears, ambitions, and murmurings that lead us to be impatient. I think that such a struggle is life-long for most of us. Although the urgency of mindfulness was impressed upon me many years ago in the novitiate, I still am not very good at it, and with every new circumstance, I tend to relapse into old impulsive ways. Perhaps the project of writing this letter is one of God's ways of telling me that I must persevere patiently in this struggle. The endeavor to be mindful amid fears and worries certainly has its good fruits. First of all, I can come to appreciate the preciousness of all human life, including the unborn, the infirm, and the criminal, both the repentant and the unrepentant. Every person who comes to my attention is a gift from God, helping me to deepen my communion with Christ. It is not for my own advantage or convenience that I encounter others but to glorify God and to extend His Kingdom of love. Besides, when I realize what a hard time I have following Christ, who am I to judge anyone, even the worst of criminals? Secondly, any task that the Lord has given me is just as precious as any other; from tying one's shoe to taking one's medicine to delivering a speech before millions, all are God's vehicles for a person to draw closer to Him and to serve others in love. Why, then, should I murmur that a task is useless and irrelevant, or why should my mind fret over all the other things that I think I should be doing or that are coming up in the next few moments? It is the correcting of an error, retrieving a lost disk, brushing my teeth, or eating a meal that God has assigned to me now, not for my convenience or selfish advantage, but (insofar as I am striving to do God's will and thus fulfilling His call to me) for His glory and the ultimate good of all mankind. Doing each task with focus and the gift of inner joy (even if outwardly I cannot help feeling discontented) will help to remind me that God wants me to be *here* at *this* task right now; so I need not be impatient for the next moment or the next task, however more valuable I may judge it to be. Furthermore, I should know how warped my sense of judgment can be in such matters. Impatience, in a sense, says, "I have a better way than the way that God has set before me. This difficulty has nothing redemptive about it; so I can murmur to my heart's content." How irreverent are such thoughts!

❧

Yes, challenges to our patience can become opportunities to rejoice. As Saint Paul tells, "Rejoice in hope, endure in affliction and persevere in prayer" (Rom 12:12). By our baptism we have all been pledged to "offer [our] bodies as a living sacrifice, holy and pleasing to God" (Rom 12:1). Let us learn from Our Lord Himself and from saints like Saint Paul that we can, with grace, learn to act "with patient endurance amid trials, difficulties, distresses, beatings, imprisonments, and riots...; [amid these we conduct] ourselves with innocence, knowledge, and patience, in the Holy Spirit, in sincere love" (2 Cor 6:4-6†).

16

ACCEPTING LOSS OF CONTROL
WITH HUMILITY AND LEARNING
TO PLACE HOPE IN GOD ALONE

Pondering the ultimate realities of death and eternal life may come naturally during autumn and on All Saints Day and All Souls Day. The fragility and imperfections of life on this earth are realities that may impinge upon our consciousness in a particular way at this time. All of us are vulnerable; all of us are broken in body, mind, and soul; all of us are moving toward death in a manner that is largely out of our control.

*

Putting together an Oblate newsletter is, for me, an example of the uncontrollability of events that prevent us from succeeding in our way and in our time. Almost every time I begin to write, I fear having too few ideas; but by the time I finish I generally have far too much to say for the newsletter's limited space. When I was composing the previous issue, the computer in my office began to make strange errors; some expected help did not come through; and (as usual) I did not meet my self-imposed deadline. Furthermore, every proofreading exposed more errors. All these chronic problems left me feeling downcast over the seemingly endless flaws of the project. With the help of God's grace, I realized once again that I had a choice: to throw up my hands in near despair and lament that things never seem to go my way, or to embrace the option of faith and humility that leaves control in God's hands, with a deeper trust that He does marvels through our limitations if only we are honest about accepting them and offering them to Him. Christ teaches us the way of childlike humility that leads to peace amid human flaws, to openness to the grace that can put together the scrambled pieces of our human endeavors, and to a growing capacity to let go of our prideful, frenzied efforts to make everything perfect by our myopic human standards. Indeed, is it not our task and our vocation to glorify God in all things rather than to seek human glory through impressive achievements? Of course, this does not mean that we should be lazy or lax in our use of God's gifts; but it does mean that even when we do our best, our results are still poor and flawed in comparison to God's magnificent splendor.

∾

In reflecting how few things we can really control in our personal lives, we are likely to develop more compassion for others whose lives are in disorder. When compiling another newsletter, I decided that everything had to be done by a certain date since I would be away giving a retreat immediately following the deadline. With that goal in mind, I felt frustrated when I received four pieces of information for the newsletter on the day of my self-imposed deadline. (Normally, I would welcome such information; but because I had made my deadline, the additional material was less than welcome.) Needing to keep everything *under control*, I frantically inserted the new material and asked another monk to take the master copy to the Mailing and Duplicating Office because I had to depart for the retreat in short time. During the retreat I had enough free time to write some 40 letters and hoped that life would be easier for me once I returned to Saint Vincent. Well, on returning to my office, I found matters very much *out of control* again: there were many phone messages; there was a large pile of unopened mail; and there had been two real tragedies in the Oblate community. Because of other immediate demands, a week later most of the mail (and, of course, then the pile was even larger) still remained unopened. Once more I faced the critical choice: to rant and rave about having so little control over my work and my schedule or, with God's grace, to learn yet again to accept things as they were as part of God's good plan for me and to follow the wisdom of the *Holy Rule*: "Place your hope in God alone."[1] Such an attitude not only tends to bring us peace but also nurtures greater compassion for others. I realized that those suffering from the tragedies carried far heavier burdens than I, with my worries about the newsletter and piles of work—relatively petty things.

℆

Anyone who has read through the *Rule* will surely notice that many circumstances in Saint Benedict's monastery are less than ideal. An abbot must sometimes deal with "a restive and disobedient flock,"[2] some of whom may be "negligent and disdainful."[3] Having undertaken "a difficult and demanding burden,"[4] the abbot may be tempted to "show too great concern for the fleeting and temporal things of this world"[5] and to worry about the "lack of [spiritual] resources."[6] A monk may be inclined to "follow his own heart's desire"[7] or to "contend with his abbot defiantly."[8] In their practice of obedience, monks may at times be "cringing or sluggish or half-hearted"[9] and respond to commands by grumbling or other signs of unwillingness. Some monks may tend to violate rules of silence,[10] and some may even indulge in "vulgarity and gossip."[11] Officials such as deans,[12] cellarers,[13] infirmarians,[14] and priors[15] may become proud, greedy, wasteful, or

1	RB 4:41
2	RB 2:28
3	RB 2:25
4	RB 2:31
5	RB 2:33
6	RB 2:35
7	RB 3:8
8	RB 3:9
9	RB 5:14
10	RB 42:9
11	RB 6:8
12	RB 21:5
13	RB 31:2
14	RB 36:10
15	RB 65:2

negligent of their duties. All of these situations are mentioned in the *Rule* undoubtedly because Saint Benedict experienced them in his communities or heard of them in other monastic communities. Each disordered situation calls for some sort of corrective measure according to the God-given responsibilities of authorities and offenders; but the non-ideal conditions also summon the abbot and community to the deep humility of acknowledging that no matter how many human remedies are applied, the monastery will still remain a refuge for weak, incomplete, sinful human beings who likewise come from a world that is very dysfunctional. Accepting such chronically ingrained imperfection requires a good dose of humility, which demands a frequent surrender of these problems to God. Like the tax collector in Saint Luke's Gospel we might often cry out, "O God, be merciful to me, a sinner" (Lk 18:13).

۵

In his book *With Burning Hearts: A Meditation on Eucharistic Life*,[16] Father Henry J.M. Nouwen, S.J., speaks of the many losses we experience in life as we grow older. He suggests that the greatest losses involve our faith:

> *As we grow older we discover that what supported us for so many years—prayer, worship, sacraments, community life, and a clear knowledge of God's guiding love—has lost its grip on us.* (p. 26)

Nouwen recommends that we should not ignore our losses or become resentful over them but rather mourn them. Remembering the Beatitude "Blessed are those who mourn," we can begin to receive comfort from God even while pain from the loss remains. Knowing that we may be responsible for some of our losses, we need to cry out for mercy rather than to complain or blame; our brokenness is part of the brokenness of the world. Finally, coming to the Eucharist with a humble, contrite heart, we allow our hearts to be "broken open,

---

16   Orbis Books. Maryknoll, NY: 1994.

to receive the water of God's grace" (p. 33). Nouwen concludes his chapter "Mourning Our Losses" by reflecting:

> *Yes, we are sinners, hopeless sinners; everything is lost and nothing is left of our hopes and dreams. Still, there is a voice: 'My grace is enough for you'...* (p. 35)

ℰ�

How, then, can we broken, imperfect people living in broken, imperfect families and communities, with situations often falling out of control, better welcome the graces that give us not only comfort but also new hope and meaning amid the messy and even tragic circumstances of life? Humility, persistent prayer, and placing our hope in God alone can help us to advance to the heights of holiness that God desires for us.

Practicing humility does not mean that I know myself to be hopeless and worthless so that I may as well give up on improving. It means that while I acknowledge that I am broken and sinful, God's lavish graces are constantly summoning me out of my self-absorption. Whenever I come before Christ in humble acceptance of my misery, which is caused in part by my self-centeredness, He draws me out of myself and leads me to rejoice in His compassionate care for me. (True joy always leads us out of ourselves!) He teaches me that there are reasons for thanksgiving, praise, and joy even amid the worst of afflictions and injustices[17] because our losses and miseries can (and should) motivate us to place all control into the hands of "Him who so greatly loved us."[18] Thus the practice of humility stirs our hearts to make Christ the true Lord of our lives.

Humility, however, will not help us to advance very far unless we *persist* in being humble and *persist* in prayer no matter how dry or empty it may feel. Blessed Mother Teresa of Calcutta endured some 50 years of inner darkness and yet persisted in faith, persisted in prayer, and persisted in a radiant charity that was surely driven by God and that moved the hearts of millions of people. Most of us

---

17   RB 7:35-39
18   Rom 8:37; RB 7:39

will never experience such prolonged darkness; yet Blessed Teresa's life gives us all encouragement to persevere in prayer amid the un-anticipated adversities of life. Rather than proudly trying to repair everything instantly, we need to welcome the grace to accept imper-fections day after day, with trust that God works wonders through our inadequacies. Our Lord told us a parable about the need to "pray always without becoming weary" (Lk 18:1). That powerful word of God assures us that He will always enable us to remain prayerfully united to Him. On our own we could never "pray always"; but with grace and our humble admission that we can't pray for even one sec-ond on our own, the Holy Spirit will groan in us and pray in us and work marvels of conversion in our hearts. And is that not what prayer is really all about: not good feelings but deeper trust and greater open-ness to ongoing conversion in the love of Christ?

Finally, along with the persistent practice of humility, we need to stop placing our hopes in things other than God. Perhaps this *task* is a most difficult one since even with good motives we can easily set our mind and heart on finishing a project, on succeeding in remembering something, on gaining someone's favor, on enjoying some possession or event or food, or even on advancing in some virtue. In some in-stances, we may not recognize pride for what it is because we are setting our hopes on something that is good or even necessary.

In my case, I often resolve to respond to some letters promptly, to go to Midday Prayer 20 minutes early, to finish a certain essay today, to complete reading a certain book by next week, or to match everyone who wants a prayer partner within a month. However, these resolutions may not be God's will for me. Unforeseen special assign-ments, mail that needs immediate attention, unexpected guests, someone's death, or my own physical or mental limitations can read-ily set my plans awry. Then I must acknowledge how much hope I have placed in fulfilling my goals and how foolishly I told myself, "I shall not be happy unless I satisfy this self-imposed expectation." Once again, I must let go and pray that I may learn better to place my hope in God alone and not in human achievements, no matter how well-intentioned.

Of course, I should mention that there is a certain good and healthful control over our sinful impulses. Placing our hope in God does not mean that we exert no human effort, especially in matters of sin and virtue. Certainly we must often say "No" to sinful impulses and take very firm measures to nurture growth in the virtues. Such necessary controls, however, are done in cooperation with grace and are not guaranteed means to overcome a fault or develop a virtue. The result must always be in God's hands lest we be caught up in a vicious cycle of self-fulfillment, even in spiritual matters, which ultimately leads nowhere instead of to a deepening relationship with God.

∾

Some day we are going to die, and what will be the benefit of our accomplishments if we have not trusted in God and done our tasks with love, the love that springs from the life of Christ within us? That love flows best when we humbly accept our human inadequacy and place our hope in God alone. Let us daily learn to let go of our prideful ambitions, to admit that some of our hopes may not be inspired by God, and to welcome the lavish graces that make our lives far more glorious than merely human strivings. Then, eager each day for the conversions that are incited by grace, we shall be prepared for the great conversion that God has in store when He leads us from death to eternal life.

17

LOSING EVERYTHING
FOR THE SAKE OF FINDING CHRIST

LOSING and finding, loss and gain are an inescapable part of life. They are also essential dimensions of the Gospel and the *Rule* of Saint Benedict. Our Lord proclaims, "Whoever wishes to save his life will lose it, but whoever loses his life for my sake will find it" (Mt 16:25).

❧

During the past few months I have been losing things more than usual. After attending an excellent afternoon theological lecture, I deposited my hat and scarf in an uncustomary place and later could not find them. As a result, I was utterly preoccupied with finding them until the next morning. On another occasion I misplaced the slips of paper on which I record several days of my daily schedule and prayer intentions. I experienced that loss as such a crisis that I found myself searching for the lost item through a large garbage container. Fortunately, they finally appeared somewhere else. I have also been in the habit of losing the old towels that I use as back supports when I am in a car. These tend not to reappear, though by the grace of God I seem to find replacements on our monastery's "beggars' bench" very readily. In all these ordinary experiences our longing to find what is lost may symbolize a deeper longing for stability, which can be found ultimately only in Christ. These very typical losses can be openings to grace when we realize—once we can laugh at our frantic searching—that God has been with us all along and is offering us something far more valuable than the thing that we have lost.

❧

The fear of losing time or wasting time can be an even more intense preoccupation. Before a recent Oblate day of recollection and monthly meeting (both at Saint Emma Retreat House), I decided to be efficient with my time by loading the car a day in advance, before I set out for a Saturday-evening Mass. As it turned out, the trunk of the car must have leaked; when I unloaded the boxes the next day, all the bottoms were wet, and some materials were soaked with water. That experience reminded me of the untrusting attitude of the Israelites in the desert when, disobeying the command of Moses, they saved some manna overnight instead of trusting that the Lord would give a fresh supply the next day. The Scriptures tell us, "When some kept a part of it over until the following morning, it became wormy and rotten. Therefore Moses was displeased with them" (Ex 16:20).

When we become preoccupied with not losing what we have, with finding what we have lost, or with providing for our future to the last detail, we, in a sense, become "wormy and rotten." We end up trusting in our own power. We end up losing what is most important, namely our relationship with God and our capacity to trust and love. We end up wasting our attention on fleeting things and not paying attention to the God who alone is all trustworthy. We end up changing directions according to our whimsical desires instead of living in *conversatio morum* according to God's ever-present call, which leads us forward in the way that is truly best for us. What can and should legitimately preoccupy us is Christ Himself. In Him we possess everything. Saint Paul proclaims, "Whatever gains I had, these I have come to consider a loss—because of Christ. More than that, I even consider everything as a loss because of the supreme good of knowing Christ Jesus my Lord. For his sake, I have accepted the loss of all things and I consider them so much rubbish, that I may gain Christ and be found in him, not having any righteousness of my own based on the law but that which comes through faith in Christ" (Phil 3:7-9). We too need to lose many attitudes, attachments, and things if we are to give our lives totally to Christ, who gave His life unreservedly to us. Father Demetrius Dumm, O.S.B., has written, "... the true role of the Christian ... [is to find] happiness simply by the seemingly foolish way of filling with love the empty spaces of need that are forever appearing among us. ... For such persons, concern for personal happiness is no longer primary and may even seem almost irrelevant."[1]

℘

The *Rule* of Saint Benedict is designed to form monks—and Oblates—as disciples committed to seeking God in Christ more and more. The commitment to stability summons the monk to be rooted in Christ alone and thus to put aside his personal agendas in order to embrace the call of God wherever it comes, whether in the Scriptures, in Sacred Tradition, in the teachings of the Church, in the commands of his abbot, in the customs of his community, or in the needs of his brothers in community. Thus he must often "lose," or leave behind, what he previously thought important, those ephemeral things in which he tried to find security. Likewise, in *conversatio morum* (which may be taken as "fidelity to monastic life" or "ongoing conversion according to monastic values"), the monk yearns daily for the growth that will enable Christ to live more deeply within his whole being. In humility, he knows how unhappy and disordered his life is; but he also acknowledges how abundantly grace can transform his life in God's own time when he takes *conversatio* seriously.

Right from the start, a candidate for monastic life is challenged to let go of illusions as he perseveres in knocking at the door for four or five days and shows himself "patient in bearing with his harsh treatment and difficulty of entry."[2] If nothing else, he surely loses the idea that a monastery is heaven on earth. After he perseveres as a novice for a year and makes vows, he must leave behind all possessions "[by giving] them to the poor beforehand, or [by making] a formal donation of them to the monastery, without keeping back a single thing for himself."[3] Yes, the newly vowed monk finds joy in knowing "that

1   *Cherish Christ Above All Else.* Paulist Press: 1996. p. 70.
2   RB 58:3
3   RB 58:24

from that day he will not have even his own body at his disposal."[4] He rejoices in being "stripped of everything of his own that he is wearing and clothed in what belongs to the monastery."[5] The monastic habit represents a new and fuller life in Christ. Thus the new monk rejoices in losing his own clothes and losing his own will insofar as he is finding Christ and striving to make Christ his all. In the paradox of the Cross, earthly loss becomes a joyful gain of heavenly treasure!

જ

How, then, are we today called to lose ourselves in order to gain Christ? First, on a theoretical level, it is good to realize that life is full of losses, some chosen and some unchosen; but in every case the acceptance of loss in union with Christ opens us to a fuller share in His divine life so that, in Him, we become blessed with great gain. If we deliberately choose to leave behind something out of love for Christ and/or out of love for others, then our very choice is a participation in the mission of Christ. If we patiently accept a loss over which we have no control, then we share in Christ's Passion, by which He made Himself an offering of love when He was delivered up into the hands of evil men. In fact, *every* choice involves leaving behind other options; so we are always losing something when we choose. Every breath we take involves some loss because our physical organism, despite occasional improvements, is headed toward decay and death. Both in the case of a chosen loss and in the case of an inevitable loss, we can actively surrender in and with Christ in a spirit of joyful acceptance and thus gain a fuller share of eternal life with Him.

Yes, every choice involves a loss of previous options, and such choices can be good and grace-filled despite the pain involved. If I become a vowed monk, I lose the options of having my own possessions and of following my own whims. If I take marriage vows, I leave behind the option of dating other prospective spouses. If I become a Catholic Christian, I no longer can choose options that go against the basic teachings of the Church in such areas as Mass attendance, obedience to the Pope and bishops, and a host of moral issues ranging

---

4   RB 58:25
5   RB 58:26

from abortion to respect for the environment. I can say that I can have it both ways, as many people do today; but it won't work. Being a Christian means that there are certain areas in which I no longer have valid options since God has made His will definitively known. Even in the areas in which I have legitimate choices, I need to make these choices discerningly, according to the Father's will as revealed in Christ. From all such "losses" emerges our true freedom as children of God. When, in union with Christ, we choose to give up our comfort and convenience and self-willed attitudes, we find ourselves taking up our crosses and gaining eternal life. We can learn to "lose" all with joy. Even the prospect of death becomes an occasion of rejoicing, not so much because I may be leaving behind a wretched, pain-racked body but because I am dying with Christ in order to rise with Him to the fullness of life in His love.

Secondly, on a practical level, the *Rule* can help us greatly when we are tempted to fret over past decisions or to worry endlessly about what we may suffer in the future. Our stability in Christ leads us to turn to Him to overcome worries and fears. The commitment to *conversatio morum* leads us to welcome Christ to reorient us in His direction in every situation and to know that His direction for us is the best. For example, when I entered the car on a recent Saturday, I belatedly discovered that it was 84 degrees outside and even warmer in the car. Since I was dressed far too warmly and it was too late for me to change my clothes, I was sorely tempted to fret; on the other hand, I could choose to surrender my discomfort (which was actually rather minor) to Christ and bear with it patiently. In the end, the Lord made it easy to forget about being too warm after I arrived in the church and prayed Vespers, took time for quiet prayer, celebrated Mass, and heard confessions. There were too many important things to do to let me remember that I was terribly warm. The next day my watch stopped during our meeting at Saint Emma, and I discovered that fact just in time for us to end the meeting and to join the sisters for Compline at 7:30. How marvelous! God gave the grace to notice the watch at the right time, the grace for someone else to know the correct time, and the grace for all of us to "lose" our rather lively discussion in mid-course so that we could do His work of praying the Divine Office. What great gain He gives us in every loss!

❧

During the Easter Season we read in the Acts of the Apostles how the first disciples let go of their past way of life and their past baggage in order to follow the risen Christ and proclaim His Good News. They learned to be joyful over these losses because they trusted in the gain of a deeper relationship with Christ. In one instance, after being whipped and ordered not to speak of Jesus, the apostles "left the presence of the Sanhedrin, rejoicing that they had been found worthy to suffer dishonor for the sake of the name [of Jesus]" (Acts 5:41). In a like manner let us, in stability, put on the mind of Christ and take up our crosses in union with Him and, in *conversatio*, welcome Christ to lead us where He will for the sake of our sanctification. In finding Christ, we have found everything, and even in our greatest losses we are privileged to reflect His glory of self-emptying love. Let us, therefore, rejoice!

18

THE GLORY OF GOD:
SHINING THROUGH OUR HUMAN WEAKNESS

THE glory of God can shine even through the gloom of a
Saturday morning in Lent when things start "going wrong"
at 3:00 A.M. The first reading at Mass on the day I have in
mind included the passage, "If you bestow your bread on the hungry
and satisfy the afflicted, then light shall rise for you in the darkness,
and the gloom shall become for you like midday" (Is 58:10). When I
reflected on these words the day before, the phrase "light shall arise"
(with Christ being the real Light) struck me as having special significance, but I wasn't sure how. Then, when I awoke in the morning
with a painful sinus headache, there didn't seem to be much light to
dispel my gloom. Furthermore, when I went to expose the Blessed
Sacrament in the chapel where we have daily early-morning expo-
sition, my cantankerous mood became even worse when I couldn't
find the usual corporal and the little stand for the small monstrance,
and I was further dismayed upon seeing a decent candle in the trash.
Although these frustrations weighed upon my sagging spirits, I mus-
tered the ingenuity to borrow a corporal from a near-by table, to
fetch a hymn book to raise the monstrance to the required height,
and to employ the resurrected candle to shine upon the exposed host.
After all that, I certainly did not expect much consolation from my
time of adoration. Within a few minutes, however, a deep and rare
peace encompassed me. (It surely came, at least in part, from the
sinus medication's taking effect; but even so, I feel it was a matter

of grace, which can work through properly taken medicine and all sorts of other earthly phenomena.) I then realized, to my joy, that Our Lord, so imperfectly displayed on the altar, did not mind such a makeshift arrangement. He was so poor and humble as to accept that awkward set-up (like the manger of His earliest days on earth), to accept my own impoverished disposition, and likewise to accept all the abysmal messiness of human life; and He chooses to shine upon it all and through it all to lavish His loving kindness upon us and to lift us up to share His own divine life. How wonderful! How immensely kind of our incarnate Lord and God! He whose glory was so profoundly manifested on the Cross does not seek to cling to any earthly glory but is eager to share His glory with us as part of His marvelous relationship with the Father.

Later in the morning I opened a letter from a person in need, who expressed a great need for spiritual literature and who was also asking for "spiritual pen pals" besides me and a way to begin a search for his missing child. By 9:30 A.M. I was able to find at least one volunteer to write to the person, to contact a search organization, and to consider what Catholic reading materials I might send to the person. Indeed, the glory of God in the Blessed Sacrament was not meant merely to give me a precious inner glow; Our Lord was sharing with me His radiant life of love so that I might "bestow bread on the hungry and satisfy the afflicted." And thus Christ chooses to work in us to shine into all sorts of situations of darkness and emptiness.

જ

The *Rule* of Saint Benedict offers us plenty of imperfect, unredeemed human situations that can function, as it were, as magnets for the glory and healing love of God. It is Christ's glory to send His Spirit to rush in, to heal, to redeem, and to call weak humans to be instruments of His work of salvation. In Prol:29-30, we are reminded that the credit for our good deeds, which are essential to any Christian life, must go to God alone. How awesome it is that we are honored to "praise the Lord working in [us], and say with the Prophet: 'Not to us, Lord, not to us but to your name give glory'" (Ps 115:1). Likewise, Saint Paul says, "Whoever boasts, should boast in the Lord"

(2 Cor 10:17). Actually, it is very freeing that we need not and ought not boast in ourselves, but rather "judge it is the Lord's power"[1] that brings about such results. How gracious of Him to invite us to do our part! When a monk is tempted to go off on his own tangent concerning penances, he is reminded that "whatever is undertaken without the permission of the spiritual father will be reckoned as presumption and vainglory, not deserving a reward."[2] When monk-artisans make products to be sold, they must be careful not to "[become] puffed up by [their] skillfulness,"[3] not to "practice any fraud,"[4] and not to be avaricious in setting prices.[5] By setting prices a little lower than those set in the outside world, the monks help to guarantee "that in all things God may be glorified."[6] Although the word "glory" is not often used elsewhere in the Rule (except to indicate the "Glory be" recited in community prayers), we may properly conclude that wherever monks humble themselves and leave behind their own disordered inclinations in order to do God's will, then God is indeed glorified.

Thus, when the abbot avoids favoritism but seeks to love all his monks equally,[7] there is the glory of God. When ex-slaves are treated with the same dignity as men who were born free (including former nobles),[8] there is the glory of God. When monks "lay down whatever they have in hand"[9] in order to obey a superior promptly, there is the glory of God, and here is an especially significant step towards "the glory of everlasting life."[10] When monks shun even "good or holy or constructive... talk"[11] because God calls them to a silence that will better open the way for them to hear His voice, there is the glory of God. When monks "are patient amid hardships and unjust

---

1	RB Prologue:30
2	RB 49:9
3	RB 57:2
4	RB 57:4
5	RB 57:7
6	1 Pt 4:11; RB 57:9
7	RB 2:16-17
8	RB 2:18
9	RB 5:8
10	RB 5:3
11	RB 6:3

treatment"[12] and thus identify themselves with Christ, who was obedient unto death, there is the glory of God. When sick brothers are "patiently borne with"[13] because they are "served out of honor for God,"[14] there is the glory of God and a very special manifestation of Christ. Again and again, whenever the monk, by grace, overcomes selfish, ambitious inclinations to conform himself in love to the self-emptying ways of Christ, there is the glory God shining out amid human frailty and the ordinariness and daily struggles.

℘

During the Easter Season we are all called to be especially aware of the glory of our risen Lord as we sing alleluias at liturgy and discover Him eating with us, calling us to fish in unpromising waters, sending us to tell the Good News of His Resurrection to people who may not really care to listen, and urging us to be witnesses to Him to the ends of the earth even when we feel utterly incompetent to do so. How can we allow His glory to become more manifest in our conscious choices and actions? When all sorts of disappointments come our way and we choose not to murmur, there is Christ in glory at our side with His all-patient love. When we are asked to let go of some "important" work in order to mop floors, there is Christ in glory working beside us. When we seek the "spiritual heights" but find ourselves in emotional and physical depths and acknowledge how much we need salvation, there is Christ in glory pouring salve into our wounds. When the delightful work that we have begun must be interrupted or transferred to someone else, there is Christ in glory, reminding us that His glory lies in humility. Yes, whenever our adversities lead us to acknowledge our human inadequacy and to place our messy situations into the realm of God's grace, then we can exult with Saint Paul and all the saints, "But it behooves us to glory in the Cross of our Lord Jesus Christ, in Whom is our salvation, life and resurrection, by Whom we are saved and delivered."[15]

---

12   RB 7:42
13   RB 36:5
14   RB 36:4
15   Antiphon for Holy Thursday and Exaltation of the Holy Cross

Therefore, let us be aware of the ways in which God's glory shines through situations of our human weakness, frustration, and disappointment—and especially during the Easter Season. It is His grace that redirects our misguided, prideful efforts, that gives us new hope when we feel hopeless, and that surprises us with the life of the risen Christ in our midst when we fear that all is gloom and doom. As Saint Paul tells us, "If the ministry of condemnation was glorious, the ministry of righteousness will abound much more in glory... If what was going to fade was glorious, how much more will what endures be glorious... All of us, gazing with unveiled faces on the glory of the Lord, are being transformed into the same image from glory to glory, as from the Lord who is the Spirit" (2 Cor 3:9,11,18).

19

THE SLOW, ONGOING DEATH-TO-SELF: OBEDIENCE IN LITTLE THINGS

As I wrote this letter, our monastic community underwent the shock of the sudden death of a young brother. We have thus experienced eight deaths of monks in one year. Such frequency of funerals gives us an opportunity to be mindful of Saint Benedict's injunction, "Day by day remind yourself that you are going to die."[1] Rather than conjuring up a gloomy image of returning to dust, such a remembrance of death, which is an essential part of any Christ-centered life of faith, necessarily ties into the complementary injunction, "Yearn for everlasting life with holy desire."[2] This daily refocusing on death and eternal life is also expressed in the baptismal summons to die daily to self and to rise daily to new life in Christ.

The disciple thus makes more and more room for Christ and shares even now in the "treasure in heaven" (Mk 10:21) and the crown of eternal life[3] that Our Lord longs to bestow on us. Saint Benedict insists that one who seeks to be humble "loves not his own will nor takes pleasure in the satisfaction of his desires; rather he shall imitate by his actions that saying of the Lord: 'I have come not to do my own will, but the will of him who sent me.'"[4] Such a disciple also "submits to his superior in all obedience for the love of God,

---

1	RB 4:47
2	RB 4:46
3	RB 7:33
4	RB 7:31-32

imitating the Lord of whom the Apostle says: 'He became obedient even to death.'"[5] Such death to self-will is a participation in the obedience of Christ and in His sacrificial death. Such death to self-will is an essential means to eternal life with Christ. Such death to self-will implies moment-to-moment obedience to whatever the Lord is asking from us in matters large and small.

Sometimes it is the small matters of obedience that are the most difficult, perhaps because we are tempted to think, "Oh, that's such an insignificant decision; it doesn't really matter how I choose"; and yet the Lord often makes it very clear how we are to follow Him in such little things. When it seems likely that one of our monks is about to die, I find myself worrying, "How shall I adjust my schedule for a funeral? I have too many things to do to put together a funeral program right now. I hope we don't have a vigil service that interferes with our forthcoming Oblate meeting." It is then that I must die to my plans and projects (as if I had any control over life and death!) and trustingly accept the Lord's timetable for death and His easy yoke for me of doing whatever He asks through superiors, *confreres*, others who may need me, and events as they succeed one another as part of the mystery of His loving plan.

Such occasions also reveal to me how deeply rooted self-will can be. Even though I have ample evidence that the Lord has carried me marvelously through undesirable changes in the past, and even though I have discovered again and again the futility of fretting over the destruction of my plans, and even though He has shown me on many occasions that His end result was (of course!) far better than anything I could have envisioned, I nonetheless tend to cling to the self-centered ways that let me feel deceptively comfortable and secure. How I need to say, "Begone!" to such worries as I dash them against Christ; and when it comes, for example, to assembling a funeral program, how I must hasten to do this task and immediately lay aside everything else, without dawdling even for a moment in the pastures that captivate me as seemingly more pleasant!

ↀ

---

5   RB 7:34

In another instance of death to self, I recently became lost while trying to find a church in a city not familiar to me. It had been my plan to arrive amply early to have time for personal prayer and to be ready to hear confessions (even though they had not been part of my instructions). As it turned out, I wandered about the city for about 40 minutes until I stopped at a gasoline station in a dilapidated section of town and was graciously served by the kind attendant, who dropped everything of his own to attend to my urgent need and gave me directions with a generous waving of his hands outside the store (and without my buying anything).

I arrived at the beautiful church still early enough to be oriented for the Mass by parishioners serving as ministers. As I calmed down later and reflected on the whole event, I realized that I had to "die" to my schedule in order to acknowledge dependence on someone else's guidance (and also the Lord's!) and to accept the wholehearted help that the Lord's servant lavished upon me. Perhaps the Lord preferred that I accept this unmerited gift, amid the frustration of being lost, rather than that I arrive at my destination through a perfectly orchestrated trip achieved, so it might seem, without His grace or anyone else's help. Just as the caring attendant dropped everything to help me, must I not abandon my plans at a moment's notice, die to every remnant of self-will, and embrace the Lord's call to a deeper relationship, especially when I see how circumstances prevent my agenda from being fulfilled?

❧

Saint Benedict's *Holy Rule* speaks often of the redemptive (and essential) value of giving up self-will. When a monk professes vows,[6] he is "to be stripped of everything of his own that he is wearing and clothed in what belongs to the monastery"[7] since "from that day he will not have even his own body as his disposal."[8] God's will, communicated through the abbot and the community, must henceforth triumph over self-will. When a monk receives any token or gift, he

---

6   RB 58
7   RB 58:26
8   RB 58:25

must immediately tell the abbot and not appropriate the item unless permission is granted.[9] When a guest arrives, other tasks are to be relinquished so that "the superior and the brothers [can] meet him with all the courtesy of love."[10]

In prohibiting private ownership, Saint Benedict reminds his monks that they "may not have the free disposal even of their own bodies and wills";[11] thus non-possession is both a concrete embodiment and a most suitable symbol of the principle of surrendering everything to God, most especially self-will.

"Unhesitating obedience" is the "first step of humility" in *RB* 5:1, even while in *RB* 7 the first step is expressed as continual mindfulness of God, which also entails that "we are forbidden to do our own will";[12] and the second step is that one "love not his own will nor take pleasure in the satisfaction of his desires."[13]

In each case the monk is to die to self-will and to embrace some new situation as God's will, bringing him new life in Christ. Such little deaths also occur in the abbot's avoidance of favoritism,[14] in the abbot's prompt correction of faults "as soon as they begin to sprout,"[15] in a monk's not following "his own heart's desire" in communal matters,[16] and in the monk's frequent opportunities to restrain speech at "times when [even] good words are to be left unsaid out of esteem for silence."[17]

All these occasions of reining in self-will promise to help to build up a community of mutual love, in which each one pursues not "what he judges better for himself, but instead, what he judges better for someone else."[18] Such restraints likewise lead one to be receptive to the "treasure in heaven," a deepening relationship with God, that Our Lord offers to the rich young man (Mt 19:21)—and to all of us who

9   RB 54:1-2
10   RB 53:3
11   RB 33:4
12   RB 7:19
13   RB 7:31
14   RB 2:16
15   RB 2:26
16   RB 3:8
17   RB 6:2
18   RB 72:7

are yet steeped in the spurious "riches" of self-will, self-fulfillment, and self-determination.

જી

How are people to practice death to self-will outside the walls of the monastery in an age and in an atmosphere in which "self" (often involving "doing whatever I feel like doing") is glorified as a god? Every day provides ample opportunities to welcome the grace to abandon self-will. One can learn to accept interruptions at work as blessings, with a wholehearted turning away from our projects in order to treat someone as a precious guest, if only for a moment. At times for prayer or Mass (when one's work is not an urgent priority of charity), one can struggle against the tendency to do "just one more thing" and decide instead to hasten promptly to fulfill the commitment to pray.

One can learn to accept corrections readily and even to savor opportunities to renounce one's bad habit at the reminder of a family member or co-worker, even if his or her manner of correction is not the most gracious. A parent can, lovingly and gently, correct a child's fault as soon as it surfaces. A lay person can formulate a personal rule of silence, especially for times when the impulse arises to curse or to lash out against someone. One can refrain from taking the last portion of some food at table when someone else might want it. One can examine one's closet and decide to donate a surplus of clothes to the poor, especially if the clothes cater to one's vanity. One can exercise restraint in the supermarket or mall when an attractive item (or package) captures one's fancy even though the purchase is unnecessary. One can turn away from an alluring invitation to spend an evening away from home if one has decided to make fellowship at table with family a high priority. In all of these instances, death to self-will, painful though it may be, opens the way for God's grace to strengthen relationships with Him and with others to whom one is committed.

In our self-indulgent culture that promotes mindless giving in to self-will without restraint, "death to self" can be difficult and painful, particularly when one begins to curb an appetite that has long been unrestrained. However, we are assured by Saint Benedict—and by Christ Himself—that abandoning what is immediately gratifying in order to follow Our Lord more perfectly will earn us "a hundred times more" than anything we have relinquished and furthermore bestow on us an inheritance of "eternal life" (Mt 19:29). This death to self and rising to new life in Christ is precisely what our Christian pilgrimage is all about.

When we confront self-will or experience the deaths of our loved ones and are reminded of the ever-present possibility of our own deaths, let us set our priorities straight. Let us embrace the love of Christ above all else and trust that by dying from moment to moment to whatever interferes with our love for Him we shall "quickly arrive at that perfect love of God which casts out fear."[19]

---

19   RB 7:67

20

STABILITY VERSUS RESTLESSNESS: ARE WE STAYING WITH CHRIST OR FLEEING FROM HIM?

A T a recent Mass, the Gospel was Saint John's version of the call of the first disciples of Jesus. After Andrew and John began to follow Our Lord, He turned and asked them, "What are you looking for?" They in turn asked Him, "Where are you staying?" Jesus responded, "Come, and you will see." The account continues, "So they went and saw where [Jesus] was staying, and they stayed with Him that day" (all quotes from Jn 1:37-39). We know that "day" was no mere 24 hours; it represented the disciples' whole remaining earthly lives and more. Despite often wavering in their commitment to Christ, the disciples ultimately persevered in remaining rooted in Him, in following Him where He led them, and in proclaiming Him courageously, even to the point of persecution and (except in Saint John's case) a martyr's death. The disciples learned to be stable in Christ from His own stability—that of "resting" in the Father's love. They learned to stop looking for self-centered advantages in order to look for Christ alone and whatever He asked of them.

☙

Staying with anything or anyone is especially difficult in our restless society. We tend to look for whatever gives us instant gratification and to flee from that which is tedious and not immediately rewarding. Influenced by the media and our fleshly desires, we seek to buy something new, to move to a new location, to switch jobs, to taste new foods, to try new styles of prayer, and even to abandon old relationships in favor of new ones, largely because we become restless with our present situation and think that happiness may come with something new and exciting. Do we then become happy? No! In fact, we can become even unhappier in our restless search for an unattainable self-chosen paradise since, in fact, authentic joy comes as a gift from God, accompanying surrender to His loving plan. Granted that God does at times call us to change (as Our Lord does in the above Gospel passage), we can easily ignore or evade His call for genuine conversion and instead pursue the superficial changes that cater to our self-indulgent whims. Only the stable commitments that are rooted in the sacrificial love of Christ can make us fully happy—i.e., joyful in fulfilling the vocation that God holds before us amid the tedium (and occasional excitement) of daily life. By fleeing the tedium of one responsibility after another, we are ultimately fleeing from God.

Whenever I write an Oblate newsletter, for example, there are moments of felt zeal (these energize the project, thanks be to God!), and there are moments of undesirable tedium, which are far more numerous. Therefore, when I do not feel especially motivated, I must overcome discouragement with a persistent trust in God's supportive presence and His saving power. In a sense, the dull moments can even help me to look for Christ rather than for self-gratification. The same applies to the proofreading of successive drafts (I wonder, "Why must there always be more errors?"), to the Saturday-afternoon task of dusting my monastic cell (I question, "What's the use of removing dust that will be back again next week? Can this really be part of God's loving plan for me?"), or to the facing of any duty when we may feel listless or exhausted. Amid our restless worries about what will become of us if we are taxed beyond our strength, we must realize that if indeed God wants us to do something, He will give us the grace to do it.

Once, on a Sunday, I faced the choice of visiting classes between two Masses. Although I felt physically and mentally weary and preferred to relax and pray in the church, I decided to make the somewhat-expected visits. Well, not only did I find the energy and grace to visit three or four classes, but also (to my great surprise) I felt more alert and cheerful after I had spoken in the classrooms, despite the characteristic unresponsiveness of most of the older pupils. While we cannot expect or demand such surprises of grace, they are vivid reminders that Christ's healing hand is always stretching out to us, both in misery and in joy, and that in any situation we should choose to put His grace to work to the utmost, without regard for our restless longings for an easy, comfortable way out. That's not to say that we do not genuinely need times for rest or prayer. At such times we should say "No" to optional commitments that prevent us from resting or praying.

ༀ

In his book *St. Benedict and St. Thérèse*,[1] Dwight Longenecker has some valuable insights into stability. Referring to the gyrovagues,[2] he writes:

> *Benedict paints a vivid portrait of the bored soul. He is a spiritual channel-hopper, always looking for the next stimulus, the next religious entertainment, the next spiritual thrill. Benedict would not reserve his condemnation for discontented monks. Church shopping is one of the spiritual diseases of our age... Benedict sees a spiritual disease underneath this physical restlessness. The disease is discontent, and it is caused by disobedience. We are born with the instinct to be our own masters; we imagine all authority to be authoritarian and do everything to avoid its claims over us... Our capacity for self-deception is so great that it is very possible to imagine we are searching for God when, in fact, we are fleeing from him with all our energy. Without stability and a superior authority we are more likely to find a god of our own making than the God who made us. We need to settle down and center down. The vow of stability is the discipline that ensures we are pilgrims and not fugitives. Benedict says: 'Commit your-*

1   Gracewing: 2002.
2   RB 1

self. Make a vow of stability and find reality, even if the reality is grim.' (pp. 98-99)

Although the *Rule* does not often use the word "stability," there are ample references to the monk's need to be alone with God, to face himself in solitude, to persevere in his God-given task with detachment from his own desires, and to trust in God's loving assistance at all times. In the Prologue, Saint Benedict cautions that the Christian "not be daunted immediately by fear and run away from the road that leads to salvation," which is "bound to be narrow at the outset."[3] He further explains that monks should never swerve from God's instructions but faithfully observe His teaching in the monastery until death.[4] The abbot must at times faithfully shepherd "a restive and disobedient flock,"[5] and he must not relent in patient acceptance of this heavy responsibility. Since one way to escape the harsh reality of the moment is to engage in critical or cynical speech, Saint Benedict reminds the disciple that "in a flood of words you will not avoid sin"[6] and that "we absolutely condemn in all places any vulgarity and gossip."[7] The gyrovagues are condemned because they are "always on the move, they never settle down, and are slaves to their own wills and gross appetites."[8] The faithful cenobitic monk, on the other hand, seeks no glamour or glory in his work but "does only what is endorsed by the common rule of the monastery and the example set by his superiors."[9] Likewise the cellarer is not to choose his own domain of responsibilities, which could lead to prideful control over others and over the goods of the community, but "should take care of all that the abbot entrusts to him, and not presume to do what the abbot has forbidden."[10] A monk who is "assigned a burdensome task"

---

3   RB Prologue:48
4   RB Prologue:50
5   RB 2:8
6   RB 6:4
7   RB 6:8
8   RB 1:11
9   RB 7:55
10   RB 31:15

should accept the order "with complete gentleness and obedience."[11] If the burden really seems too cumbersome, he may prudently appeal to the superior; but if the superior holds to his order, the monk "must in love obey" as he "trusts in God's help."[12]

Perseverance in difficult tasks is possible because of God's lavish help. His gracious assistance often works through the discipline of "not fleeing." It is grace that keeps us faithful to the difficult task or relationship that we must confront in a certain place and at a certain time. Our baptismal promises, our monastic vows, and our Oblate commitments bind us to remain firm because of God's unshakable promises. In taking monastic vows, a monk promises not "to shake from his neck the yoke of the rule which, in the course of so prolonged a period of reflection, he was free either to reject or to accept."[13] Oblates likewise commit themselves not to flee from the spiritual practices of the *Rule*, if indeed the Lord has called them to such a commitment. By baptism all Christians are pledged to take on the yoke of Christ, which means to die and raise daily with Him and to persevere in the often-burdensome project of ongoing conversion, purification, and repentance from sin. Rather than to flee from the yoke of Christ in any particular situation, the Christian is to flee (in Latin *fugientes*) "the torments of hell,"[14] "shun [(*fugere*)] arrogance,"[15] and flee (*fugiat*) forgetfulness of God.[16] Thus, in any given situation, we might ask ourselves, "Am I to flee into a mindless pursuit of my own whims, or am I to flee to God?" Our faith assures us that He comes to us and calls us through legitimate daily responsibilities, however tedious; but do we want Him to show the way? Thus we might also ask ourselves, using Our Lord's words from Saint John's Gospel, "What am I looking for?"

The mysteries of Christmas and of Lent can help us in our quest to stand firm. In the "holy exchange" of Christmas, as one of the Christmas prefaces at Mass tells us, "God became one with man so

---

11	RB 68:1
12	RB 68:5
13	RB 58:16
14	RB Prologue:42
15	RB 4:69
16	RB 7:10

that man might become one with God." Even before He endured the Cross, Our Lord embraced the routine nature of ordinary life in order to sanctify it and make it for us a pathway to eternal life with the Father. As the Letter to the Hebrews tells us, "Since the children share in blood and flesh, [Jesus] likewise shared in them, that through death He might destroy the one who has the power of death, that is, the devil, and free those who through fear of death had been subject to slavery all their life" (Heb 2:14-15). Yes, the devil urges us to flee, to give up, and to become discouraged with the tedium of life because it wears us out and seems to lead to death. In contrast, Jesus, both by embracing the tedium and by dying on the Cross, encourages us to embrace the "little deaths" of our dull routines because He shares them with us, fills them with grace, and can thus use our stability in God-given tasks to further the salvation of the world. Our dull, wearying work, in fact, becomes His work!

✑

How, then, can we better look for Christ and flee to Him amid our daily routines and minor decisions as well as in our long-range decisions? Stability can certainly help us. If we are considering making a certain change, we might again ask ourselves, "What am I looking for?" Are we tempted to flee from something merely because it is not glorious and glamorous and because we want something more fulfilling, self-promoting, affirming, or scenic? We should be cautious about leaving a task, a location, or a relationship only because we think we shall feel better after the change; it might very well be an escape from something that God has given us. When we have a choice, does the contemplated change promote the Kingdom of God, or does it promote mainly our self-interest? Yes, God does sometimes call us to improve our material or emotional lot, but there are also many tedious or trial-filled situations that we cannot escape (although we underhandedly try to by murmuring and blaming), as well as those situations from which we should not escape. Not to feel good about what we are doing is no crime! When we discern that we are to stick with a certain task, a certain location, or a certain relationship, we can tap into the grace to persevere by frequent prayer and perhaps by the repetition of a psalm verse. Some that come to mind are: "His help is near for those who fear him" (Ps 85:10[17]), "To you I stretch out my hands" (Ps 88:10[271]), and "Show forth your servants" (Ps 90:16[271]). Saint Paul tells us, "Let us not grow tired of doing good, for in due time we shall reap our harvest, if we do not give up" (Gal 6:9). Armed with graces flowing from the word of God, we can let go of distracting thoughts and emotions that tempt us to go elsewhere. As an overflow from our praying of the Liturgy of the Hours and from our *lectio divina*, we can welcome God's word—and the very Word of God, Jesus Christ—to rush in to fix our hearts and minds on what the Lord, in His wisdom, has given us to do. The key idea is to do just one thing at a time; we cannot really focus on more than one task anyway; so why do we keep trying to do five things at once? If you are like me, I think I must have control over the next task and the one after that, and if I don't scheme to regulate every detail of the future now, I might be doomed to fail. Such an attitude, however, leaves little room for trust in God and further divides our already scattered attention.

When the restlessness of trying to do multiple tasks at once overcomes us, we need to pray, "Lord, help me to do well this one task that You have given me; I give You all my restlessness for healing; I need not try to make myself more important by taking on many things, for Your love already sustains me amply in this one little task." In union with Christ, let us offer up our tedious tasks to the Father and know in faith that as He does with our Offertory gifts at Mass, so He does with the substance of our everyday lives, whether pleasant or unpleasant. In this wondrous exchange, as we give Him the work of our human hands, God gives us the grace of renewed strength to pursue our tasks, the wisdom to stand firm and not to flee, the inclination to submit to Christ and not to our self-indulgent impulses, and the very life of Christ Himself. How could we wish to flee from anything as beautiful and glorious as that?

17   Grail Psalter. GIA Publications. Chicago: 1963

21

The Call to Hospitality:
Often Ordinary and Draining,
Sometimes Unrewarding,
but Always Glorious

SOMETIMES writing this article, like many tasks in life, feels like a dull, unrewarding duty. As I begin this reflection, I am tempted to lament that I am not swept up with any particular inspiration and that I am not feeling my best physically, mentally, or spiritually. Also, as I ponder the course of these past few days in early October, I feel that I have been bearing with a succession of tasks that have not shown much promise. I've been trying to recover a listing of Oblate library books after I somehow wiped out the former listing on an old computer. I've been wondering why my computer disk caused some college computers to "freeze." I've been continuing a seemingly endless project of cutting and pasting pages of music for an ongoing revision of our Divine Office. And one day I found myself asking, "Why?" as I pushed a food-service cart down several hallways to pick up boxes of programs and deliver them to their proper places. What is the meaning of all this dreary, uninspiring routine, often accentuated by physical weariness and mental confusion?

A few notable occurrences amid the drudgery reminded me that "something more" was happening. One employee responded generously to a request that I made of her but also shared how greatly physical ailments were weighing her down. Was I not being called to stir up some prayerful compassion for her? Another person very patiently examined a year-end report of the Oblate account, about which I had inquired for clarification. (Alas, even simple financial reports utterly baffle me.) Did she not merit my lavish thanks and praise after I had foolishly "made much ado about nothing"? Then an Oblate approached me with his need for prayers as he prepared to face surgery the next day. Was this not also a sacred encounter summoning me to prayerful attentiveness? In the course of several days other people reminded me of a week-long fast for the Pro-Life cause sponsored by our seminary. Could not *my* small sacrifices be part of that urgent cause? All these little incidents awakened me to the truth that the succession of my apparently insignificant tasks meant far more than "getting things done." In the reality of God's Kingdom each step of each task involved a challenge from God Himself to deliver my work into His hands, to make each deed a sacrificial offering to Him, and to know in faith that even the most routine duty is a wonderful opportunity to be hospitable to others and to provide them with loving service, whether visible or hidden. Of course, to practice such hospitality requires sufficient time for prayer, in which we come to know the loving hospitality of God Himself, Who alone can give us the grace to share His divine hospitality with others.

The sacredness of ordinary tasks also can become manifest when we are away from home. During my summer vacations for several years, I had the privilege and convenience of staying overnight at another monastery on the way to visit my mother in Upstate New York. For obvious reasons the slowed-down pace away from Saint Vincent helped me to appreciate the beauty of encounters that I might tend to ignore back home at the Archabbey. For example, as I carried my overstuffed bundles of luggage through the guest entrance, a woman kindly opened doors for me. She turned out to be a long-time friend of the community. As I thanked her, I thought of asking her something about herself, and she proceeded to tell me about her children, one after the other, and of their need for prayers. In committing myself to pray for them and for her, I realized how important it was to pay attention to such people and their needs. By stopping to enter into others' concerns and burdens, we can strengthen the eternal bonds of love that Christ has already established among us but which we are responsible to make *concrete* within the limited time and energy we have in this world. In short, we are called to hospitality in the most ordinary and unpretentious situations as well as in seemingly larger matters. Signs of hospitality at unexpected moments from the monks also touched me during my brief stays at the monastery, where I considered it a great privilege to have my offer to help with small after-meal tasks accepted. Why, oh why, I thought, am I blind to such opportunities at home, where I see myself as so overburdened that I miss the blessing of being asked to perform any extra service? Are we not serving the same Lord, whether at home or away from home? In any case, my peace-filled hours at the monastery helped me to maintain a certain sense of tranquility as I drove on the road, and when I stopped at a gas station and was gently told by another customer, "There's a dead bird on your front grill," I saw that even this not-so-welcome message encompassed another little act of hospitality, a concerned reaching-out from a stranger, a grace, a gift. Now I know that the gracious concern that I experience as coming from God when I am *away from home* is meant to make me more sensitive to such blessings when I am *at home* so that I, too, may become a better instrument of divine hospitality amid the less glamorous settings of our daily common life. That is no simple endeavor; it is the struggle to keep loving and serving amid the stability and routine of community or family!

℘

The *Rule* is often cited for promoting a long-standing tradition of "Benedictine hospitality" to guests. Special care is to be shown in receiving "poor people and pilgrims, because in them more particularly Christ is received."[1] The monks are to meet guests "with all the courtesy of love."[2] A visiting monk is to "be received for as long a time as he wishes," and even his criticisms, if reasonable, are to be heeded carefully as possible messages from the Lord.[3] The porter is always

1   RB 53:15
2   RB 53:3
3   RB 61:3-4

to be available to visitors with a spirit of gratitude for their presence and is to speak to them "with the warmth of love."[4] Furthermore, if we examine the *Rule* as a whole, there is also much evidence for the regular practice of hospitable service among the monks themselves amid the routines of everyday life. "The brothers should serve one another."[5] The abbot, the cellarer, and other monks should be highly concerned that the sick "truly be served as Christ."[6] All the brothers are quietly to encourage one another on arising for the Work of God.[7] The abbot, using *senpectae*, is to serve even "the wavering brother" with such a hospitable loving outreach that he may be gently encouraged to reform his life and not be overwhelmed by excessive sorrow.[8] Thus the routines and chores and problems of everyday life in the monastery provide innumerable opportunities for mutual hospitality as the monks compete in showing respect to others, bear patiently with one another's weaknesses, and show one another "the pure love of brothers."[9]

❧

This call to faithful, hospitable service applies to *all* of us, even amid the unrewarding and often draining tasks of daily life. For one thing, even when we are working alone, the care and reverence that we put into our work render it a genuine service of hospitality to Christ, to those affected by our work, and ultimately to all the members of Christ's Body. An occasional glance at Our Lord and a reflection on who we are and what we are doing can help us to function in light of this wonderful truth. Serving with love when we are alone can prepare us to recognize time spent with others as a sacred opportunity for extending ourselves in hospitality. When someone comes into my presence, I can make an effort to look at that person with genuine concern, at least for a few moments, and can wish a blessing upon him or her in as unhurried a way as possible. When someone

---

4	RB 66:2-4
5	RB 35:1
6	RB 36:1, 10
7	RB 22:8
8	RB 27:2-3
9	RB 72:4-8

shows signs of weariness or illness, I can ready myself to share his or her burdens and promise prayers in a way that is genuinely caring. When someone bears patiently with *me* in my sometimes confused or foolish requests, then I can awaken myself to a spirit of sincere thanks and praise, offer some heartfelt affirmation in response to the generous help, and resolve to treat others with the same patience and generosity even when my self-centered impulses may cry out, "This is silly. I can't waste *my* time doing this!" (And who am I to say that any moment of time is *mine?*) Might it not be the Lord Who summons us to stretch ourselves to do some dull, unrewarding task; Who actually works *in* us as we try to put some love into the "daily grind"; and Who Himself receives hospitality and service in the person whom we help?

Yes, even when our day feels routine or dreary, even when our tasks seem draining and unrewarding, God's unfailing grace, offered with lavish, loving hospitality, can renew us in a wholehearted commitment to serve Him and others. Our feeble efforts to cooperate with that grace become glorious stepping-stones to eternity insofar as we unite them to the Cross of Christ. Perhaps the less glamorous the task, the greater the opportunity we have to plunge in with love and to entrust the whole "mess" to the Lord when we ourselves feel so uninspired and inadequate. Our Lord Himself reminds us that when we "have done all [we] have been commanded," we are to say, "We are [useless] servants: we have done what we were obliged to do" (Lk 17:10). Since God has done everything for us in Christ, why should *we* seek credit or glamour or glory or guaranteed success according to *our* preconceived notions? At the same time, Our Lord *does* come to infuse our routine tasks with divine life. Yes, on this troubled earth and in our humble abodes, He chooses to enter our houses and dine with us and have us dine with Him (Rev 3:20); He invites us to sit on His throne of victory with His Father (Rev 3:21); and He even deigns to serve us as we are seated at *His* table (Lk 22:27-30). What unsurpassable hospitality! How could we fail to pass on that hospitality to others, without thought of glamour, glory, or reward?

22

⬤

SILENCE, POVERTY OF SPIRIT, AND WEAKNESS: UNDERVALUED TREASURES

THE practice of silence can help us to realize that, while we should, out of love for God and for others, try our best at anything that we do, our every effort is necessarily flawed and imperfect.

☙

Recently, I had the luxury of having much quiet time to myself in a parish rectory, during which I savored a book, *Poverty of Spirit*, donated by one of our Oblates, and I read it almost all the way through. The book focuses on "poverty" as part of the essence of being human. We are essentially poor because we are incomplete and still being recreated by God to become the fully loving children that He intends us to be. In the meantime, it is poverty of spirit that opens us to acknowledge our inherent weaknesses along with an abundance of God's graces; it is poverty of spirit that also binds us together as weak, struggling creatures seeking communion with one another in Christ; it is poverty of spirit that moves us forward on the path of conversion as we keep longing for completion in union with God, Who is our only hope for salvation and ultimate perfection. Yes, thank God for our poverty![1]

---

1   Johannes B. Metz. Paulist Press. Mahwah, NJ: 1968, 1998.

Subsequent experiences of my failure to embrace poverty taught me how much silence is a necessary disposition for nurturing poverty of spirit. How often we use noise—both inner and outer—to keep ourselves living in the illusion of being rich, self-sufficient, and righteous. After an annual medical check-up I found myself murmuring with dissatisfaction over a good report; then I perceived my hidden desire for the doctor to find some little thing wrong so that I could overcome the poverty of not feeling perfectly well! Some time later, while another monk and I were reading Sunday newspapers, I made a brief comment about what he seemed to be reading so intently; when he then began to talk on and on about a subject that I could not understand, I regretted that I had opened such a "can of worms." That is, I did not want to feel the poverty of looking and feeling ignorant and unable to share someone's avid interest. (Of course, I really should have said a brief prayer, "Lord, in my poverty and weakness, help me to share his interest as best I can!") On other occasions I have blamed myself for feeling dry and empty when I had some much-cherished time for quiet prayer; I blamed myself because I was avoiding the poverty of accepting my discomfort and empty-handedness before God. On the other hand, I tend to forget how God occasionally interrupts my dry, distracted prayer by calling me to serve someone's urgent need. Little does the other person know what a grace and blessing he is providing. It is sometimes in my misery that I can better appreciate God's call to serve others through this frail earthen vessel. In all these instances, the quieting of our inner noises and the embracing of silence can lead us to put to a halt our diverse schemes that dishonestly deny our poverty; such a practice of silence can also open us to welcome the reality of poverty and weakness as vehicles of God's saving intervention. As Saint Paul tells us, "We who live are constantly being given up to death for the sake of Jesus, so that the life of Jesus may be manifested in our mortal flesh" (2 Cor 4:11), and "when I am weak, then I am strong" (2 Cor 12:10).

☙

The *Rule* of Saint Benedict encourages us to have "esteem for silence," so that at times even "good words are to be left unsaid."[2] It also exhorts us, "Monks should diligently cultivate silence at all times, but especially at night."[3] Why is it that silence must be so esteemed and cultivated? As is so often said in spiritual writings, silence is to be sought for the purpose of listening; and in Benedictine life this listening is to be directed especially to discerning the saving presence and loving call of God in every situation. We are to ask, "How is God here, and what is He asking of me?" instead of, "What am I to get out of this?" or "How can I glorify myself in this situation?" Some outer silence is necessary in every Christian life to make way for some inner silence, or stillness, that enables us to be in touch with God, beyond our noisy, impulsive reactions and even in and through them. With inner silence, we can enjoy Christ's gift of peace even when there is much turmoil around us. In fact, only with some silence can we truly pray. Saint Benedict stipulates that "after the Work of God, all should leave [the oratory] in complete silence and with reverence for God"[4] so that others may be free to pray and, presumably, so that the spirit of silence will continue into the activities that follow one's prayer in the oratory. With that silence we can speak to others "with the warmth of love."[5] With that silence we can accept a task that we prefer not to do "with complete gentleness and obedience"[6] or "explain patiently... the reasons why [we] cannot perform the task."[7] With that silence we can move quickly and work assiduously and yet approach our community prayer and our work "with gravity and without giving occasion for frivolity."[8] Perhaps most importantly, with silence we can accept our weakness and poverty without becoming discouraged or defensive. The *Rule* has abundant examples of correcting one's faults, changing one's plans, restraining one's selfish desires, and adjusting one's outlook by taking counsel with others. All

2   RB 6:2
3   RB 42:1
4   RB 52:2
5   RB 66:4
6   RB 68:1
7   RB 68:2
8   RB 43:2

of these necessary processes become part of our spiritual journey because they arise from humble recognition of our essential inadequacy and our need to turn to God to find an alternative, more loving way to deal with situations. (To achieve this, He often works through other people.) Without silence, we are likely to murmur and rebel at anything that threatens our individualistic preferences, pompous ideas, self-righteous behaviors, and false sense of security.

જ્જ

It is important to realize, too, that a proper understanding of Christ-centered silence helps us know how and when to speak. My writing about silence was motivated partially by a letter from a correspondent who had resolved to take a "vow of silence," as he thought we monks do. (To set the record straight, although silence is a necessary and basic monastic practice, monks do not take a "vow of silence"!) Thinking that his decision was imprudent, I searched through my files in vain for an article on "Benedictine silence"; and so I decided to write this letter. The silent pondering of my friend's situation led me to "speak out," at least in writing; and he decided that it was his call to witness by speaking prudently rather than to vow silence. Likewise, during a recent meal with some of our new novices, some efforts at inner silence helped me to restrain my impatience to depart quickly for my work and instead to stay and benefit from the novices' valuable insights about the significant countercultural atmosphere of the monastery. The practice of silence moved me to slow down inwardly, to be engaged in others' precious sharing, to contribute a few words of my own, and, in the end, to benefit from a renewed appreciation of a blessing that I tended to overlook. Praise God!

જ્જ

How, practically, can we nurture a spirit of silence that will help us to embrace our essential poverty as God's gift and to accept our weaknesses as stepping stones that hasten us on the journey to be one with Christ? Two suggestions come to mind. Our inner noises tend to become apparent in our times of prayer, when we may be tempted to become discouraged over the multitude of distractions. The existence

of such inner noises does not prevent us from praying or being inwardly silent; only giving in to them does. Therefore, our Christian
task is not to fight the distractions but to renew our focus on Christ,
simply and humbly. Amid myriad undesirable thoughts and feelings,
we need to know that God accepts us in our miserable poverty and
is very ready to break through the mess to embrace us even when
we feel no consolation. We need to stop blaming ourselves (or other
people or circumstances) and instead persist in saying, in one way or
another, "Here we are, Lord, You and I. You know I am miserably distracted! I know I'm too weak to fight these distractions on my own;
so I'm doing my best not to focus on them, no matter how often they
keep coming back. Rather, I give them all to You while I rest humbly
and in need in Your hands amid all the noise. You can take care of
these; and if I simply persist in not wanting them, Your grace will
cleanse and heal my disturbed heart in marvelous ways!"

Secondly, we can learn to eliminate sources of outer noise in our
lives that threaten our practice of silence and keep us from accepting
our poverty and weakness. After we have said something angry or defensive, we can step back and recognize how we used haughty speech
as a screen to hide from God and from our own judgmental tendencies; and thus we can repent and try to be better next time. After we
have indulged in some mindless form of noisy entertainment, we can
ask ourselves, "Do I really need that sort of social activity or recreation? Does that noisy activity really bring me closer to God?" Again,
we can repent and resolve to stay away from such unnecessary outer
distraction. After we find ourselves "undisciplined and restless"[9] at
some task, we can ask ourselves if we worked too long or too in-
tensely, with self-centered success as an addictive goal. If so, we can
repent and discern how we need to put restraints on our overindul-
gence in work. After we experience indigestion from an over-hasty
meal, we may be able to discover why we were in a hurry and thus
failed to appreciate both the gift of food and the gift of the people
around us. (We may have said grace, but perhaps we did not let grace
pervade the meal because of our inner noises and outward haste!)

---

9   RB 2:25

Once again, we can repent and discern how we can slow down, when possible, and not be so intent on rushing from one thing to another.

❧

May our body and soul work together, then, to nurture inner and outer silence, so that we may better conform to our "divine vocation," which daily takes us through "the various steps of humility and discipline as we ascend toward God."[10] Only by descending in poverty and weakness can we ascend in love to fuller communion with Our Lord, Who humbled Himself to enter time and space to be one with us in our humanity. His times of silence in the womb of the Blessed Virgin Mary and in the obscurity of thirty years in Nazareth were a necessary part of His bringing us redemption. When we nurture silence, we come to discover Jesus Christ as our strength amid our weakness and our treasure amid our poverty. Thus we can proclaim with Saint Paul, "I will... boast most gladly of my weakness, in order that the power of Christ may dwell with me" (2 Cor 12:9).

10   RB 7:9

23

---◉---

CHANGING FROM EVIL WAYS OF THE PAST AND EMBRACING NEWNESS OF LIFE

RECENTLY there has been much new life in our monastic community. New novices were clothed with the monastic habit. Novices who entered last year professed their first vows. Furthermore we had intensive community meetings, at which we monks discussed a number of new situations in a new way. For us monks of the Archabbey, it has been a time to remember that we who live in Christ are called to "newness of life" (Rom 6:4) and summoned by God to be "transformed by the renewal of [our] mind[s]" (Rom 12:2†).

ↄ

All of us have realms where we prefer not to grow and change, even when God is calling us to move on. Several months ago my watchband disintegrated beyond repair. I thought of buying a new band, but I never found the opportunity to go shopping for one (partly because I really did not want to go out on such an errand). As a result, I learned to carry the face of the watch in my habit pocket and to take it out whenever I needed to know the time. Well, after not many weeks of living by this new routine, the watch itself stopped; so I firmly resolved to go out to buy a new battery as well as a new band. Alas, it turned out to be much cheaper to buy a whole new watch! When I first started wearing a watch on my wrist again, I found part of me longing for the "old way" of keeping the watch in my pocket. I had become accustomed to taking out the watch only when I needed it, and that routine had the benefit that I was less tempted to check the time too often. Thus even a rather new routine became a familiar way of functioning that I was reluctant to cast off.

In some circumstances we are blessed to have other people to prod us forward to growth-filled change. Recently I felt the need to purchase some new viola music to expand my repertoire. After I performed the convenient task of ordering three volumes by phone, I had to pick up the music at a store in Latrobe. When I arrived home, I realized that one volume was not the one I had ordered. I phoned the store again, and the clerk agreed to supply the correct volume in exchange. A couple of weeks later I had to drive to Latrobe once again to accomplish the transaction. That time I was blessed to find a parking space almost right across from the music store, and there was still time in the parking meter. However, the space was located between two already parked cars, and I am not skilled at parallel parking. After several minutes of twisting the car into and out of the space, I felt that I had done my best and proceeded to walk over to the store. As I did so, a man some distance away kindly cried out, "Father, you had better get your car in closer. It's sticking out too much!" Therefore, in embarrassment, I tried and tried again to park the car correctly, and I finally managed to get it a bit closer to the curb. At that point I was so frustrated that I wondered why I had ever decided to order any music. Later, however, after I had calmed down, I learned several grace-filled lessons from the incident: (1) setting out to do something new inevitably involves trials, which must be borne patiently; (2) even at my age I was able to do *something new* by improving my underdeveloped ability to do parallel parking; and (3) I should be grateful for the concerned stranger who did not want to see the car— or me—in any danger. Such ordinary adversities of daily life can be wonderful occasions of growing in "newness of life"!

༄

Saint Benedict and the Church's law require that monks profess vows of "stability, fidelity to monastic life, and obedience."[1] The second vow, *conversatio morum* in Latin, is also translated in such various ways as "ongoing conversion according to a monastic manner of life" or "the perfection of charity in a monastic way of life." The Latin phrase probably encompasses all these meanings and more. That vow, or promise in the case of Oblates, helps to keep us growing and changing through a lifetime of fidelity to the Gospel and the *Rule* as we seek to live out their values in growing charity in family and community. An Oblate or monk must never give up on growing and changing because Christ Himself beckons us to this ongoing conversion, often through disappointments and failures. Learning trustingly to leave behind things and ideas of the past and to adjust former ways of behaving is a key to this growth. The monk entering the community "is to be stripped of everything of his own that he is wearing and clothed in what belongs to the monastery."[2] These new clothes, and often a new name, symbolize the newness of life in which the monk or Oblate is always to live. Our life is no longer ours, but Christ's!

Every day, says Saint Benedict, a monk is to confess his sins to God and "change from these evil ways in the future."[3] His fellow monks challenge him to this daily conversion from self-will to self-emptying love through both encouragement and correction. The abbot is to help his monks move forward spiritually with a variety of techniques; in varying circumstances and with different individuals, he is to be "threatening and coaxing by turns, stern as a taskmaster [or] devoted and tender as only a father can be."[4] He and the other officials of the monastery assist the monks to discern the will of God, to "abandon their own will,"[5] and to turn God's will as "they follow the voice of authority in their actions."[6] Sometimes authorities knowingly or unintentionally create "difficult, unfavorable or even

---

1   RB 58:17
2   RB 58:26
3   RB 4:57
4   RB 2:24
5   RB 5:7
6   RB 5:8

unjust conditions"[7] in the community. In such situations "the faithful must endure everything, even contradiction, for the Lord's sake"[8] and thus hasten to receive a "reward from God,"[9] which includes the gift of spiritual growth that comes through adversity. The "seniors" (perhaps the deans) of the monastery have authority to warn twice privately any brother who is "found to be stubborn or disobedient or proud" or who "grumbles or in any way despises the holy rule and defies the orders of his seniors."[10] Such warnings are issued not to show disdain for the individual but to help the person to overcome deficiencies. In these and other instances, the ongoing conversion of each monk is to be nurtured. The abbot and other officials are to "hate faults but love the brothers";[11] those in charge are "not [to]... allow faults to flourish but rather... prune them away with prudence and love as [they see] best for each individual."[12]

It might do well to note that three Benedictine vows work together and, to some extent, overlap. Obedience and stability both support *conversatio morum*. Obedience tells us in which direction we are to change (not all change is positive growth), and stability challenges us to accept the sufferings involved in change with patience and rootedness in the Cross of Christ.

How, then, can we better nurture our commitment to *conversatio morum*? We might first be grateful for the areas in which—at least for the present—we are not called to change. Too much change on too many fronts, as some of us well know, can render our lives a turbulent mess! I myself like my jobs in the monastery, and I have not been called to have a change of assignment for some years. Likewise, I am content with the monastic schedule, with my weekend ministries, with my generally good health, and (on the whole) with the community as it is, and I tend not to want these things to change in any major way. Yet, at any moment, I might be summoned, by obedience or by circumstance, to let go of any of these out of love for Christ

---

7	RB 7:35
8	RB 7:38
9	RB 7:39
10	RB 23:1
11	RB 64:11
12	RB 64:14

and the Church. You or I might even be asked to embrace terminal illness or to die. If so, our commitment to *conversatio morum* tells us to let go gracefully, to embrace the cross of painful change, and to trust firmly that Our Lord will bring us to a genuine newness of life. This transformed life is better than the life that we must relinquish, if only we faithfully welcome Him to accompany us on each step of the journey to life eternal.

Aside from occasions of major change and realms where change seems not to be demanded, conversion usually happens in small, quiet ways from day to day, especially in the ordinary decisions that we make. As members of Christian communities, we are to welcome people, circumstances, and events to transform us—as God's grace works through them. In particular, we are to open ourselves to others' good advice and sometimes to seek out such counsel. Even when someone's words irritate us, we are to realize that God allowed such communication for a reason. If advice given is bad or irrelevant, then we can grow in humility by graciously accepting the person who offers it. (That, of course, does not rule out correcting someone lovingly when he or she needs to be corrected—not only so that we might feel relieved, but so that the other might grow in virtue.)

℘

After I had written a good part of this article, I had the blessing and trial of undergoing double-hernia surgery. As a result, I have had to accept various restrictions, to change my daily habits in very significant ways, and to accept others' advice about which medications to take, what to eat, how to sleep, how to stand and sit, and how (not) to climb stairs. In almost every instance, I have come to recognize the advice as very good, but following it and changing long-ingrained habits have been hard. I must trust that all these challenges are helping me to embrace newness of life in Christ as I let go (at least temporarily) of past ways—those ways that are not helpful for recovery from surgery or, in the larger picture, for a life consecrated in obedience to God.

℘

In addition to welcoming others and what they communicate to be instruments of ongoing conversion, we need to see that God sometimes calls each of us to help others to grow in Christ. Most of us have at least occasional, if not daily, opportunities to correct (lovingly), to encourage, to warn, to affirm, or to show compassionate concern and solidarity even when we do not feel like it. I am amazed how, on occasion, after I have uttered such words as "How are you feeling?", the other person launches into a ten-minute sharing of sorrows and joys. We can trust that such heartfelt outpouring and patient listening by the one who seeks to enter into the other's situation will help the troubled person to see his or her circumstances as part of God's loving plan and as part of a journey of ongoing conversion in the ways of the Gospel.

Let us rejoice, then, in all the means God uses to help us to "hasten toward [our] heavenly home."[13] The Church's teaching, the Scriptures, the Rule, our friends and family, and those in Christian fellowship with us can all help us, as God permits and arranges, toward our goal to "change from... evil ways"[14] to the ways that keep us on the path to holiness and help us to do all "out of love for Christ, good habit and delight in virtue."[15] More and more cleansed of vices and sins, we shall little by little reach the "loftier summits of... teaching and virtue"[16] set before us and thus be ready for the heavenly reward that "God has prepared for those who love Him."[17]

---

13   RB 73:8
14   RB 4:58
15   RB 7:69
16   RB 73:9
17   RB 4:77

24

OBEDIENCE WITHOUT DELAY:
PUTTING ASIDE OUR ANXIETIES
AND FINDING CHRIST'S PEACE

SOME years ago, when I was serving as a hospital chaplain, I learned to deal with a hospital pager—and to accept the value of prompt obedience that came with that little device. Although I never found it appealing to be on call, especially at night, I discovered in the summons to visit a critically ill patient or the family of someone who had just died that God provided me with abundant graces that were often very palpable. At the sound of the pager, I would typically respond with fearful expectations and some murmuring, but then on the road to the hospital I would generally recollect myself and gather the strength and zeal to serve those in need. In fact, the experiences were often deeply moving. How marvelous that the beeping sound of a mechanical device should represent the call to enter more fully into the life of God Himself and of some of His people who wanted someone to bring them a measure of His compassion! Yes, God did indeed provide. Why should I be anxious? Nevertheless, in recent months, when I was asked to carry a hospital pager on several occasions, I found myself once again becoming anxious and rebellious at the thought of being interrupted at any moment. As it turned out, the pager never did sound, but just knowing the possibility that my plans might be upset led me to think, "It just can't beep now; I simply have too much to do! No, Lord, You wouldn't interrupt me now, would You?"

In another situation this past September, while I was flying back home from Saint Bernard Abbey in Alabama, the challenge to obey instantly and to overcome self-centered anxieties again caught me off guard. As I began the journey on the first of three flights, I subtly clung to the thought that I absolutely had to arrive in Pittsburgh by 8:30 P.M. because I had to catch the 8:50 commuter plane to Latrobe in order to get a good rest in my own cell that night. Well, it didn't work out that way. After a late boarding and a delay on the ground for an hour in pouring rain, the plane from Charlotte to Pittsburgh took off an hour and a half late. What made the delay especially frustrating were the plane's repeated advances on the runway a few yards at a time, followed by further stopping. Every time the vehicle started moving, I thought, "Perhaps *now* we'll get off the ground," and then my false hopes were dashed. Ironically, I was reading a book about Our Lord's Passion,[1] and it struck me how impatiently I was bearing with my little sufferings in contrast with Our Lord's quiet embracing of unimaginable tortures. What dismayed me further was my inability to do anything to calm my rising tension and anxiety, coming from a worry that "all would be lost" if I could not arrive in Pittsburgh on time. My mental and emotional disarray undoubtedly arose from my failure to put every moment of the flight into God's hands and to accept every possible affliction with patient, trusting obedience. Since missing a connecting flight, as far as I could remember, had never happened to me before, I did not really trust that the Lord could take me through the situation in such a way that I would benefit from it. Instead, I too easily allowed the onslaught of self-centered anxieties to snuff out the peace of Christ within me until it was almost too late to regain a sense of God's faithful presence (although, of course, it's never really too late to turn back to the Lord!). (Perhaps some other time I shall relate the marvelous little blessings that arose from having to stay overnight in Pittsburgh.)

---

1   *Cross of Death, Tree of Life*. Jerome Machar, O.C.S.O. Ave Maria Press. Notre Dame, IN: 1996.

❦

The *Rule* of Saint Benedict teaches us much about obeying without delay, in the cases both of a positive summons to change one's course and of a call to bear an adversity with interior steadfastness. Saint Benedict's several exhortations to "run on the path of God's commandments"[2] in themselves enjoin the monk to a prompt, unhesitating obedience to fulfill whatever God is asking. Saint Benedict's chapter on obedience places strong emphasis on an immediate abandonment of self-will and an eager, wholehearted fulfillment of God's will without "grumbling or any reaction of unwillingness."[3] Such obedience must be both exterior and interior, with gladness in the heart, since the call to obey is an opportunity, however difficult, to show one's love and gratitude to Christ and to imitate His humility in obedience to the Father. Thus "the first step of humility is unhesitating obedience, which comes naturally to those who cherish Christ above all."[4] Instances of such unhesitating obedience are scattered throughout the *Rule*. In being summoned to the first hour of the Divine Office, "the monks will always be ready to arise without delay when the signal is given."[5] When a brother has become wayward, "it is the abbot's responsibility to have great concern and to act with all speed, discernment, and diligence"[6] to reach out compassionately to the troubled monk. The cellarer should "provide the brothers their allotted amount of food without any pride or delay."[7] If a monk commits a public fault, "he must at once come before the abbot and community"[8] in order to admit his fault and make amends. When a visitor comes to the door of the monastery, the porter is urged to praise God for the blessing brought by the person's arrival; "then, with all the gentleness that comes from the fear of God, he provides a prompt answer with the warmth of love."[9] All these circumstances

---

2   RB Prologue: 49; probably quoting from Ps 119:32
3   RB 5:14
4   RB 5:1-2
5   RB 22:6
6   RB 27:5
7   RB 31:16
8   RB 46:3
9   RB 66:4

invite the monk to prompt obedience to the call of God, coming through ordinary daily tasks and ordinary human encounters.

ℂℇ

One could say that unhesitating obedience also applies to situations in which God is calling us out of such dispositions as murmuring or other disordered thoughts. The temptations of the devil should lead the monk to "[fling] both him and his promptings far from the sight of his heart."[10] In fact, "while these temptations were still young," the zealous disciple "caught hold of them and dashed them against Christ."[317] Saint Benedict reinforces this precept in the instruments of good works: "As soon as wrongful thoughts come into your heart, dash them against Christ and disclose them to your spiritual father."[11] Since Saint Benedict warns so frequently against murmuring, this prompt surrender of evil impulses to Christ would apply most especially to grumbling over a particular adversity or an annoying person. All our anxious, self-centered impulses must yield to quick repentance and conformity to Christ's wholehearted obedience to the Father.

In what ways might prompt obedience be particularly relevant to life situations today? Reflecting on Phil 4:6-9, I sensed that anxiety is a characteristic plague of our fretful, fear-filled culture, and it needs to be dispelled quickly and frequently if we are to dwell in the peace of Christ, listen to Him eagerly, and obey Him unreservedly. Saint Paul tells us, "Have no anxiety at all" (Phil 4:6). Furthermore, if we bring our concerns to the Lord instead of anxiously holding on to them, then "the peace of God that surpasses all understanding will guard your hearts and minds in Christ Jesus" (Phil 4:7). Similarly, the priest's prayer at every Mass immediately after the Lord's Prayer includes the plea, "Protect us from all anxiety." (Perhaps here it is appropriate to comment that the word "anxiety" is often misused in place of "eagerness." In this era of the loss of accurate speech and of precise meanings, people often use "anxious" in a positive, hope-filled way when they really mean "eager." It may have been in the

---

10   RB Prologue:28
11   RB 4:50

fifth grade that teachers taught us pupils to distinguish between
"eager," involving the anticipation of something attractive, and "anxious," denoting the dreaded anticipation of something undesirable.)
As the Scriptures and the liturgy instruct us, it is never good to be
anxious. Anxiety is a disorder. Anxiety keeps us from the peace of
Christ. Anxiety enslaves us to focus on our own fears and worries.
Anxiety keeps us from doing one thing at a time with loving attention. Anxiety prevents us from listening patiently to others. Anxiety
inhibits our reaching out to share others' concerns and to meet their
genuine needs. Anxiety constricts our hearts and minds and severely
limits our capacity to hear God's word and to act upon it because
anxiety binds us to preoccupation with self. Therefore, let us dash
anxiety against Christ promptly and, if it keeps returning, surrender
it to Christ over and over. Likewise, we can strive to avoid the near
occasions of anxiety that we freely choose: trying to do more than one
task at a time, thinking of fearful scenarios of the future, dwelling on
past sins, stirring up fears about what other people think about us,
eating carelessly or "on the run," or spending time on the computer
on projects that needlessly generate worries or fears or disordered
passions. Whenever such temptations arise, we need to acknowledge
them as temptations, ask the Lord for strength to slow down and
say "No" as is appropriate, and thus end the vicious cycle of one
anxiety feeding into another. We can all benefit from heeding Saint
Benedict's admonition for abbots: "Let him strive to be loved rather
than feared. Excitable, anxious, extreme, obstinate, jealous or oversuspicious he must not be... Instead, he must show forethought and
consideration in his orders, and whether the task he assigns concerns
God or the world, he should be discerning and moderate."[12]

૨૭

When we celebrate the feasts of All Saints and All Souls and when
we see nature preparing for winter, we can rather naturally turn to
Saint Benedict's advice: "Day by day remind yourself that you are
going to die."[13] To keep death in mind daily, for us Christians, can

12   RB 64:15-17
13   RB 4:47

be refreshingly freeing insofar as it places all our human hopes and projects into proper perspective. Christ Himself shared our death and shares in our little "deaths" each day as we are weaned away from our self-will in order to surrender all to God the Father as Jesus did. Why, then, be anxious about the losses that we endure? They are all encompassed in Christ's own death, and they are meant to be stepping-stones to a share in His Resurrection. Indeed, we prepare well for our ultimate death by dying daily to self-will and rising daily to obedience to the voice of Christ, who summons us to live in His peace and in His all-generous love. Let us, then, not become so attached to any material goal that we lose sight of God's wonderful plan for us. Working for God's Kingdom rather than for our own kingdoms, we can labor without anxiety or fear because every task belongs to God, and His grace always sustains us and makes good even of our failures. Let us be among those who "are ready to give up [our] own [wills] once and for all and, armed with the strong and noble weapons of obedience, to do battle for the true King, Christ the Lord."[14] These weapons will conquer all anxiety and, along with the grace-filled steps of humility, will help us to "arrive at that perfect love of God which casts out fear."[15]

---

14   RB Prologue:3
15   RB 7:67

25

STRIVING FOR SIMPLICITY
AND REVERENCE IN SPEECH:
A CAUSE FOR HUMILITY

WHEN are we to speak, and when are we to be silent? If we speak, how are we to do so with love and in the name of Christ? To answer such questions with wisdom requires a lifetime of experience and more, and still we are susceptible to fail and to harm others in our use of speech and silence, even when we try our best. Some of the recent readings at Mass focused on hearing and speaking prophetic words. All of us, we might conclude, are called to proclaim Christ and His Kingdom; and yet to do so authentically we must first listen in silence. Our struggle to keep prudent silence and to "profess the truth in love" (Eph 4:15†) when we are called to speak should surely remind us of our dependence on God's grace and teach us humility, if nothing else.

The *Rule* of Saint Benedict urges monks to be silent in a multitude of situations and to nurture a spirit of inner silence, or recollection, that denotes persistent attentiveness to God's call. In our especially unfocused and noise-filled age, both lay people and monks could benefit much from pondering the *Rule*'s high esteem for silence. On the other hand, the practice of silence is not an end in itself. It must lead to God. A recollected silence can open into communication that is loving, reverent, and subservient to God's will, and often that communication needs to be verbal. Communicating with love is a significant dimension of our vocation as Christians, Oblates, and monks, with the degree of communication depending on our God-given roles.

೧೨

I know how frustrated I can become when I leave a significant message on voice-mail or write a letter with some urgency and then receive no reply for weeks or even months. Sometimes I receive no reply at all, or a reply that ignores the issues that I raised. (I suppose, too, that a number of people are frustrated with me for still not having e-mail!) In my frail humanity, I raise such questions as, "Did I do something to offend? Am I being rejected? Did I ask too much of someone? Has the other person undergone a personal crisis, about which he or she does not wish to share with me?" My failure to communicate has certainly hurt others, too.

Some months ago a third party told me that certain people wondered why I had not stopped to talk with them for quite a while. When I subsequently opened myself to conversation with these people instead of rushing by, I realized that some of them wanted to share urgent concerns with me and to ask for my prayers. My presence and my verbal response to them were important. In another situation I felt too rushed to tell a certain pastor that I was coming for the weekend after a switch had been made. Although I rationalized that it would not matter whether I called ahead of time or not, I later learned that phoning in advance would have been helpful. In such situations, we can see that appropriate verbal communication is a demand of charity as well as a call from God. The wrong kind of silence can be an escape from the relationships God has given us to treasure and nurture.

೧೨

Alongside its strong emphasis on silence, the *Rule* calls for good communication, even with words, at certain times and places. The abbot is to teach and command and is responsible before God for fulfilling these tasks faithfully.[1] When the brothers are summoned for counsel, they are to give their advice,[2] although they must be careful "to express their opinions with all humility."[3] Among the Instruments of Good Works is the summons to "console the sorrowing,"[4] which would normally involve words of compassion. Also, Saint Benedict recommends "moderation in speech," with "no foolish chatter";[5] appropriate speech was a normal part of life even in the very regulated monastic atmosphere of Saint Benedict's time. The cellarer surely needs to talk frequently with those who approach him with needs, and he is asked to "offer a kind word"[6] when a particular item is not available. During Lent the monks are to consider denying themselves "needless talking and idle jesting";[7] therefore, Benedict's monastery must have had times for needful talking and possibly even charitable jesting. The porter is to greet guests with such phrases of welcome as "Thanks be to God" or "Your blessing, please,"[8] and he is to respond to visitors' inquiries with "a prompt answer with the warmth of love."[9] A monk who thinks he cannot perform a burdensome task has the right to "explain patiently to his superior the reasons why he cannot perform the task,"[10] and a dialogue of discernment follows that verbal initiative. In all of these situations Saint Benedict finds loving, respectful speech to be acceptable and even desirable.

❦

The Bible offers helpful advice about simplicity and directness of speech. Especially in Saint John's Gospel, Jesus is the One who always speaks the truth that comes from the Father. At His trial He says to Pilate, "I came into this world to testify the truth" (Jn 18:37). At the Last Supper, Our Lord, assuring us of His oneness with the Father,

---

1	RB 2:4-6
2	RB 3:2
3	RB 3:4
4	RB 4:19
5	RB 4:52-53
6	RB 31:13
7	RB 49:7
8	RB 66:3
9	RB 66:4
10	RB 68:2

proclaims, "The words that I speak to you I do not speak on my own. The Father who dwells in me is doing his works" (Jn 14:10). As disciples, we are to be one with Jesus in His mission of proclaiming the truth. In His high-priestly prayer, He asks the Father to "consecrate them in the truth. Your word is truth" (Jn 17:17). In the Sermon on the Mount, Our Lord, warning against taking oaths, directs us always to speak simply and honestly: "Let your 'Yes' mean 'Yes,' and your 'No' mean 'No.'" (Mt 5:37). In Mt 6:2, He tells those who give alms to do so silently and not to advertise what they are doing. Near the end of the Sermon, Jesus criticizes those who cry out, "Lord, Lord," and boast of prophecies, exorcisms, and miracles but do not do the Father's will. Jesus Himself gives us an example of silent cooperation with the divine will at His trial, when words were futile. Saint Paul's letters are full of advice about thoughtful Christian speech, and he often warns against empty boasting. Saint Peter exhorts his people, "Sanctify Christ as Lord in your hearts. Always be ready to give an explanation to anyone who asks you for a reason for your hope, but do it with gentleness and reverence" (1 Pt 3:15-16). Thus, both Our Lord and the apostles instruct us to be simple, direct, and reverent in speech. Our hearts are to become pure with the love of Christ, and our speech should reflect that pure love as we offer information, extend encouragement, and give witness to our faith.

༧

Since good communication is so difficult, it is helpful to know what sorts of communication we need to avoid. We communicate wrongly when we fail to listen, when we try to promote our own agendas, or when we do not have reverence for the people with whom we are interacting. Our culture sometimes promotes thoughtless or manipulative communication. I thought I might find plenty of examples on billboards during my weekend journeys to parishes, but to my surprise most advertisements along a particular road seemed to speak directly and honestly about a service or product being offered. One billboard even read, "We buy ugly houses." (I suppose that the phrase is meant to attract attention!) On the other hand, I saw one billboard with the meaningless statement, "The sandwich that isn't," and another with the dangerous generalization, "Reputation is everything." (If that is so, then we must live in continual fear of what others think.) An ad in the *New York Times* asked, "Exactly how much is a piece of priceless jewelry worth?" (Are we to live in a world where a material thing is valued as priceless?) In any case, such promotions can teach us both to be on guard against biased messages in the media and to be aware of the ways in which we might be tempted to "advertise ourselves" in speech, whether by overstating our strengths (or weaknesses) or by using one of various techniques to make people think what we want them to think.

☙

In his book *A Guide to Living in the Truth: Saint Benedict's Teaching on Humility*,[11] Father Michael Casey, O.C.S.O., offers some helpful suggestions for overcoming patterns of excessive, boastful, or irreverently humorous speech and for nurturing speech that is gentle, serious, modest, brief, and reasonable. These reflections occur in his comments on Saint Benedict's ninth, tenth, and eleventh steps of humility.[12] Reverent, caring speech comes from a heart that is in loving attention to God, and so we need to seek the dispositions of "a listening heart, a quiet mind, a subdued imagination, stilled passions, [and] a body at rest" (p. 162). (Father Michael also recommends a "non-intrusive environment," but not all of us have that luxury.) The ninth step tells us that there are many times when it is better not speak at all so that one can maintain a contemplative attitude toward life. "Much conversation clouds perception," says the author; "the relentless exchange of information and opinion tends to substitute extensive knowledge for intensity of experience" (p. 164). Regarding the tenth step, on the avoidance of laughter, he says that we need not agree with Saint Benedict unreservedly, even while we do need to recognize that laughter and certain types of humor can undermine "seriousness, mindfulness, diligence, sobriety, moderation, and kindness and acceptance of others" (p. 175). Finally, the eleventh step, says the author, itemizes "the qualities of an elderly person who

11   Liguori Publications, 2001.
12   RB 7:56-61

has attained a measure of wisdom: gentle, serious, humble, grave, taciturn, low-voiced, and sparing of words" (pp. 176-177). He warns against imposing such an ideal all at once on young people, although we might certainly aspire to such ideals in the long run. Also, active lay people, relatively active monks, and contemplative monks will seek to apply such norms in varying ways.

❧

Practically speaking, then, what are we to make of all this advice? Saint Paul urges the Ephesians and all of us to avoid being caught up by the mindless spirit of this age, "by every wind of teaching arising from human trickery, from their cunning in the interests of deceitful scheming. Rather," he exhorts us, "living the truth in love, we should grow in every way into him who is the head, Christ" (Eph 4:14-15). Yes, all of our speech is to be governed by Christ's law of love. Our words should profess the truth that we are striving to live in Christ. Thus, if we are responding to someone, we need to take the other person seriously and choose words that will be helpful. If we are offering information, we must be careful to provide what really benefits the other and not what advertises our imagined extensive knowledge or our supposed status. If we are called to take the initiative to greet or console, then let it be with the warmth of Christ's love. There may also be times when we are summoned to witness explicitly to our faith. In such cases, we must rely on the Holy Spirit's guidance to proclaim Christ and His truth in a respectful way, without efforts to overwhelm or manipulate the other person for our glory. Also, we must trust enough to leave the result in God's hands.

Another suggestion comes from my experience of accompanying the choir of monks on the organ. I have learned that after giving an introduction to a hymn (or completing a verse), it is essential to pause for a moment (and not to jump into the verse right away) because the choir needs time to collect itself. Likewise in speech, instead of plunging into an over-zealous reply even before the other person finishes speaking, pausing for a moment and trying sincerely to digest what the other has said can help us to respond with gentle reverence and lead us both to discover the truth and draw closer to Christ.

❧

Having said all this about simplicity and reverence in speech, I fear that I may have been confusing and noisily irreverent in what I have written above. In any case, reflection on the way we speak can help us to conclude how easy it is to sin in speech, or at least to tend towards self-centered advancement. It is no wonder, then, that three of Saint Benedict's twelve steps of humility deal with silence and speech. Acknowledging the disorder in our *speech* can help us to recognize the pre-existing disorder in our *thoughts*; as a result, we can commit ourselves to beseech the Lord humbly and persistently for transformation of our thoughts and words into what they should be. Let us learn from the very frank reflections of Pope Saint Gregory the Great taken from a homily on Ezekiel:

> *In my position I must often communicate with worldly men. At times I let my tongue run, for if I am always severe in my judgments, the worldly will avoid me, and I can never attack them as I would. As a result I often listen patiently to chatter. And because I too am weak, I find myself drawn little by little into idle conversation, and I begin to talk freely about matters which once I would have avoided. What once I found tedious I now enjoy.*
>
> *So who am I to be a watchman, for I do not stand on the mountain of action but lie down in the valley of weakness? Truly the all-powerful Creator and Redeemer of mankind can give me in spite of my weaknesses a higher life and effective speech; because I love him, I do not spare myself in speaking of him.*[13]

---

13   From the Office of Readings for September 3.

26

Preparing for a Holy Death:
Being Put to Death Continually[1]

DEATH is inevitable. Modern technology does much to prolong life and postpone death, and much of that process is good. Modern medicine also prolongs and often enhances life by keeping at bay afflictions that would otherwise incapacitate us or cause us to die relatively early. Blessings though these human advances can be, they can also deceive us into thinking that death will never come. No matter how far medicine and technology may progress, the body necessarily weakens; our faculties lose their sharpness; our mental and physical abilities wane; and one illness or another, or some accident, will ultimately bring us to the mysterious transition called death. Yes, our bodies will eventually fall apart, usually piece by piece; God seems to have made them that way, and for a good reason (see Rom 8:20-33). As we find in our older years that we can no longer do what we did in our younger years, we can grow bitter and rant and rave, or we can surrender gracefully and look beyond the physical diminishment. We *do* have a choice of attitude. The question, then, is not *whether* we are to confront death but *how*. As followers of Christ in the way of Saint Benedict, how can we best approach the inevitable phenomenon of death in a Christ-centered way and thus render the passage into eternity a holy death?

℘

1   RB 7:38

The word "death" is used in various ways. The *Catechism of the Catholic Church* specifies three dimensions of physical death: as "the end of earthly life" (#1007), as "a consequence of sin" (#1008), and as a phenomenon "transformed by Christ" (#1009). In another use of the term, we can say that much of our society has espoused a "culture of death," with death denoting separation from God and His covenant with us. Those who espouse a culture of death often choose "spiritual death" by ignoring the realities of judgment, heaven, hell, and eternal life and the spiritual significance of physical death. Perhaps without realizing it, many persons opt for a loss of eternal values by living only for pleasure, popularity, power, and possessions. Christians, however, struggle against spiritual death by facing the reality of physical death and even embracing it insofar as Christ has transformed it. The *Catechism* tells us that the end of earthly life "lends urgency to our lives: remembering our mortality helps us realize that we have only a limited time in which to bring our lives to fulfillment" (#1007). Hence, Saint Benedict gives us the timely advice, "Day by day remind yourself that you are going to die."[2] Beyond this sense of urgency and limitation, the Christian "can transform his own death into an act of obedience and love towards the Father, after the example of Christ" (*Catechism*, #1011). Because of Christ the daily remembrance of death also becomes an occasion to "yearn for everlasting life with holy desire."[3] We who cherish Christ above all and look to the *Rule* for guidance are blessed to have means for preparing ourselves for a holy death and for the joy of everlasting life, to which death is the gateway.

This preparation entails much spiritual warfare. Saint Benedict warns us that spiritual death is an ever-present possibility even in a monastery. The abbot may have to contend with rebellious, disobedient sheep, and these "will be punished by the overwhelming power of death"[4] if they persist in willful disobedience. The persistent misuse of speech can propel a person on the way to condemnation since "the

---

2   RB 4:47
3   RB 4:46
4   RB 2:10

tongue holds the key to life and death."[5] Saint Benedict refers to the example of Ananias and Sapphira to caution us that "all who perpetuate fraud in monastery affairs [will] suffer spiritual death"[6] unless they repent. Such relevant admonitions remind us all that any stubborn disobedience, prideful abuse of the tongue, practice of fraud, or persistence in any serious sin can direct us along the path that leads to doom.

In contrast, there is a marvelous and life-giving sort of death: death to self. The persevering and grace-filled struggle against spiritual death opens us to a positive and even joyful attitude toward physical death as we prepare for it each day by denying ourselves and taking up our crosses. Because of Christ's victory over death, we can say with Saint Paul, "For to me life is Christ, and death is gain" (Phil 1:21). We can likewise proclaim, "If we have died with him we shall also live with him" (2 Tim 2:11) and even "I long to depart this life and be with Christ" (Phil 1:23). This attitude of finding in death the fulfillment of our relationship with Christ stands in contrast with the prophet Jonah's sulking after the conversion of Nineveh. He uttered in frustration, "'I knew that you are a gracious and merciful God, slow to anger, rich in clemency, loathe to punish. And now, Lord, please take my life from me; for it is better for me to die than to live'" (Jon 4:2-3). Once again, after he lost God's gift of a gourd plant, "he asked for death, saying, 'I would be better off dead than alive'" (Jon 4:8). Jonah wanted to die because he did not get his way. God had shown mercy to Jonah's enemies, and Jonah was fed up with life and its disappointments. Jonah wished to die not to encounter God but to escape from God and from his own responsibility as a prophet. Sometimes we Christians, too, may long to die for somewhat selfish reasons entailing relief from earthly frailties and trials; yet ideally we strive to anticipate death not just for relief, but more basically for the fulfillment of our communion with Christ, already begun on earth. Longing for this fellowship with Christ, we can even embrace the sufferings of purgatory, a "cleansing fire," so that we may appear in God's presence purged of sins and imperfections. As the *Catechism*

---

5   RB 6:5; quoting Prov 18:21
6   RB 57:6

teaches, "All those who die in God's grace and friendship, but still imperfectly purified, are indeed assured of their eternal salvation; but after death they undergo purification, so as to achieve the holiness necessary to enter the joy of heaven" (#1030). Because of our growing communion with Christ, we can accept with anticipatory joy, like the joy of Lent in the *Holy Rule*, the redemptive sufferings of this life and the purifying sufferings of purgatory. Little by little, death can lose its "sting" (1 Cor 15:55-56), and fear of death can fade away because of Christ's victory and our growing desire for deeper communion with Him.

The way to a holy death, whether it leads first to purgatory or directly to heaven, is to embrace cheerfully the daily "deaths" involved in ongoing conversion. This process of dying and rising with Christ, in response to God's graces, is the basis of our baptismal commitment. Thus we prepare for death and the final purification of purgatory by welcoming opportunities to die with Christ every day. It is a matter of putting to death both sin and any tendencies that prevent us from living fully in Christ. Saint Paul urges us, "You too must think of yourselves as [being] dead to sin and living for God in Christ" (Rom 6:11), and "if by the spirit you put to death the deeds of the body, you will live" (Rom 8:13). Saint Benedict asserts that zealous disciples of Christ, in their suffering and in being "put to death continually,"[7] "are so confident in their expectation of reward from God that they continue joyfully and say, 'But in all this we overcome because of him who so greatly loved us.'"[8] Every trial or frustration can thus become the occasion of a little "death" with Christ and a preparation for a full surrender at the time of physical death. When we turn to Christ in appreciation of His sacrificial love for us instead of being trapped in self-centered protest, we receive the grace to become more alive in Christ.

☙

Each day presents us with innumerable opportunities to die to self and "continue joyfully" in the way of Christ. Some time ago I glanced

---

7   RB 7:38; quoting Rom 8:36
8   RB 7:39; quoting Rom 8:37

at four books in my monastic cell that I have been taking to monthly Oblate meetings for years, even though I have not been using two of them at all during meetings. Why, then, did I continue to transport those four books month after month? Apparently the routine gave me a sense of security; it led me to think, "I'm prepared for anything; I've done my very best to get ready for the meeting." Although the matter is fairly minor, letting go of the habit of carrying those two unnecessary books gave me a new sense of freedom to rely more on God than on an outmoded routine. Dying to an unmindful practice symbolizes the many other "deaths to self" that can free us to encounter Christ more genuinely and to prepare for death itself more gracefully. When I perform a task that turns out to be useless, I can die to the impulse to blame myself. When I fail to complete all the items on my day's schedule, I can die to the tendency to pout. When an hour is "gained" with the return to standard time, I can die to the desire to plan every extra second to my personal advantage. When I work on this letter, I must die to the temptation to do other things that are less challenging, especially when I feel tired and uncreative; I must die to the craving to have it all done right away; I must die to the wish to spare myself much editing and proofreading; and I must die to the foolish dream that the end result will be error-free. Ironically when we die to self-centered desires and false hopes, we become more free and joyful in doing our work as a response to grace instead of as a burdensome task for which we are entirely responsible. We can aim to please the Lord instead of feeding our insatiable whims. At the same time, we can learn gracefully to relinquish old habits and misconceptions, to accept each little death in communion with Christ, and to embrace the new life and the hope-filled future that God has in store for us. If in faith we learn daily to die to self in response to God's promptings, then when physical death approaches, we shall be well prepared to accept the mysterious transition to purgatory and heaven, where our "I" will have been converted totally to "Christ in me."

☙

So, let us welcome the grace in *lectio divina* and other forms of prayer to "yearn for everlasting life with holy desire."[9] May longing for a holy death keep us more vigilant over the current of our thoughts so that we may consecrate them more fully to Christ and turn away more readily from sinful tendencies and old self-centered habits. As the prophet Isaiah said to King Hezekiah, "Thus says the Lord: 'Put your house in order, for you are about to die; you shall not recover'" (2 Kings 20:1). (As it turns out, Hezekiah repented, recovered, and lived for 15 more years!) In a sense, we never really recover from the diagnosis of death. Life on earth is terminal. In another sense, by dying to self in communion with Christ, we are always "recovering" from the wounds of original sin and personal sin; by dying with Christ, we are recovering our baptismal innocence ever more fully. In Christ, the arduous and inevitable decline toward death becomes a joyful advance toward the fullness of life. As Saint Paul tells us, "Death is swallowed up in victory. Where, O death, is your victory? Where, O death, is your sting?" (1 Cor 15:54-55).

---

9   RB 4:46

ABOUT THE AUTHOR

Father Donald S. Raila, O.S.B., is a Benedictine monk of Saint Vincent Archabbey in Latrobe, Pennsylvania. He has been the Director of Oblates since 1988, and during that time has written quarterly letters to the community of Oblates and friends of Saint Vincent Archabbey.

Index